storybooth

story booth

Compiled by
Marcy Kaye and Joshua Sinel

Art by David SanAngelo

HARPER TEEN
An Imprint of HarperCollinsPublishers

Dear Readers,

The book you are about to read is one hundred percent real. Its stories are told by brave teens bold enough to share a piece of themselves with the world. These are their true confessions, secrets, struggles, embarrassments, heartbreaks, and the truths that make up their lives. Every single contributor's story is told in their own words. (As always, we at Storybooth add the pictures.)

We can't promise you Instagram-perfect happy endings, but we can promise that every story included will shed some light on what makes us all human and, in doing so, help everyone to feel less alone.

We want to let you know that there are a lot of emotions in the pages ahead, and some stories cover difficult subjects.

We thank all the storytellers brave enough to share their stories with us. Your voices inspire us and remind us that we are all in this together.

HarperTeen is an imprint of HarperCollins Publishers.

Storybooth

Lettering by Colleen Bringle

For information address HarperCollins Children's Books, a division of HarperCollins Publishers, 195 Broadway, New York, NY 10007.
www.epicreads.com

Library of Congress Control Number: 2021951684
ISBN 978-0-06-305793-7

22 23 24 25 26 RTLO 10 9 8 7 6 5 4 3 2 1

First Edition

For Chloe and Jack.
Thank you for reminding us what it means to grow up
and for allowing us to see the world through your eyes.

storybooth

YOU'RE NOT ALONE has

SOME HIDE them

IT DOESN'T matter just

YOU ARE NO

EVERYONE CHALLENGES. SOME SEEK help. WHICH one you ARE, know THAT alone.

I GUESS I'M DOING THIS because I want to get this off my chest, and maybe there's someone out there who kind of feels the same. Even though I do have friends, something always weighs in the back of my mind. Do I really fit in?

I liked hanging out with my friends at school, but I never really did outside of school. I saw how all the more popular girls in my class seemed to hang out every day. It was all over Instagram, and suddenly I noticed how my own friends hung out outside of school too. At school they would still hang out with me, but I'd be thinking, *Do they really like me? Do they actually see me as a friend, or are they just being nice?* I'd lie awake in bed and worry that I was just crazy-annoying and didn't know it.

It didn't comfort me when adults I tried to talk about my problems with disregarded it and would say, "Teenagers, hormones, that's kind of what happens. Don't overthink things," which made me believe that this was just me being overdramatic.

But I just don't seem to fit in anywhere, even among my friends and family. I guess it'd be nice to find someone else like me.

THERE WAS THIS GUY I was so in love with, and I was really comfortable in the relationship.

So one day we were just texting, and he asked me, "Do you trust me?" And I said, "Yes, I trust you." And then he said, "Can you send me nudes?"

I told him, "I can't send you those type of pictures. Why would I do that?" And he said, "You say you trust me." And I said, "Yes, I trust you, but I really don't want to send parts of my body through social media." Then he was like, "Oh, you don't trust me," or "You don't love me," or whatever.

I felt as if I were on a trampoline, my feelings were up and down. But then I was like, I don't want to lose him. I was so dumb for that. And I sent them.

He broke up with me and then AirDropped pics of my boobs to the whole school.

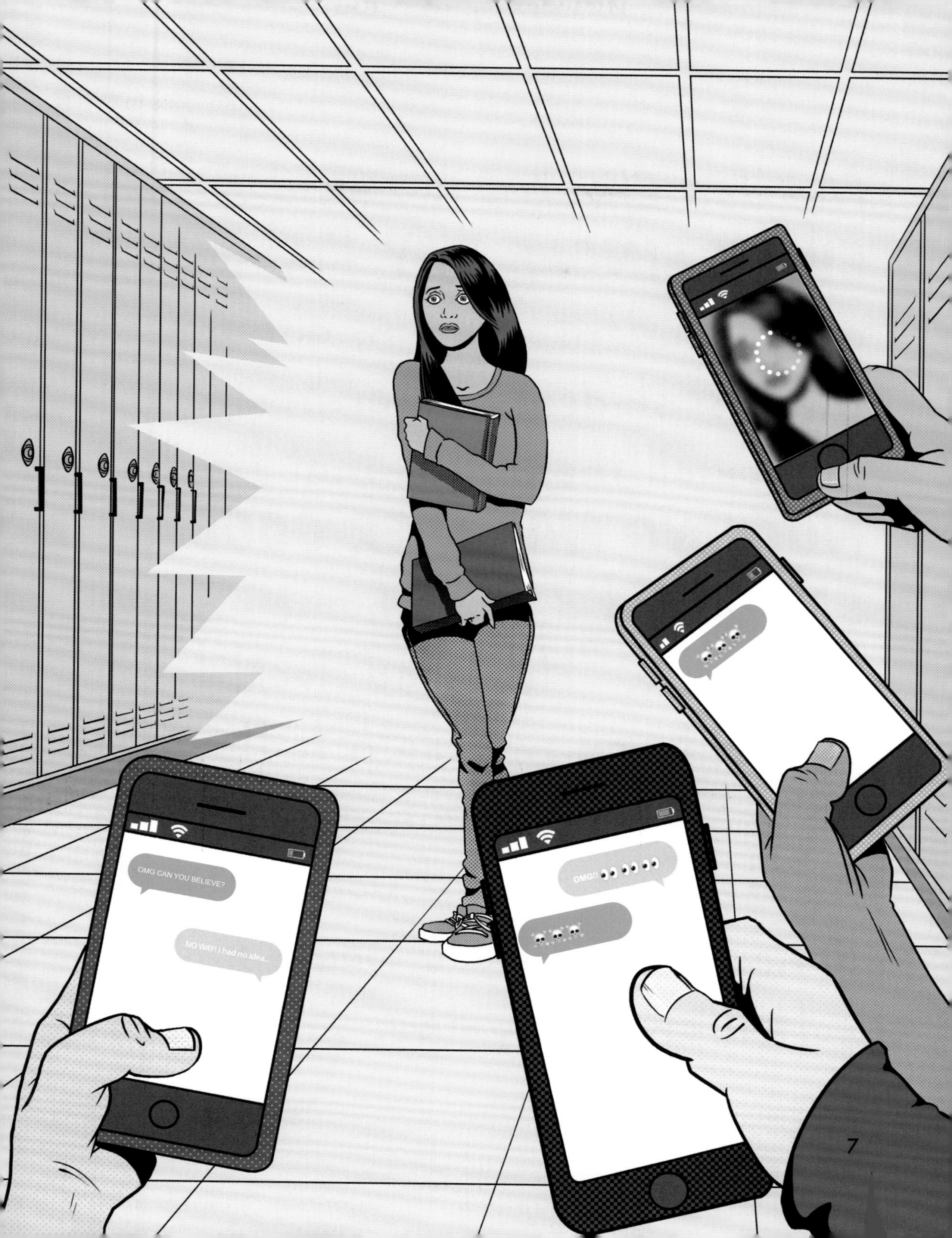
OMG CAN YOU BELIEVE?
NO WAY! I had no idea...
OMG!!

My dad checked my grades **EVERY SINGLE DAY**. I'm not a bad student, but I'm also not the best student. He criticized me for all the grades that I got. **NOTHING WAS EVER GOOD ENOUGH**. I'd come home and I'd be like, "Hey, Dad, look! I got an eighty on my math test!" He'd look at the math test, and he'd be like, "Oh, well if you had just done this, then you would have gotten an eighty-five."

THERE'S THIS PROBLEM THAT I have, and I can't help it. I am a gaming addict, which is not only bad for me but bad for my family and friends. My grades are not good. I don't want to study. I just want to play games. When I'm out with my friends, I just get hyped to go back home to play some PlayStation. I hate this about myself.

I am trying to make this better, but it is hard. I am trying to help myself, to go out with people, to play with my friends and to play sports.

Do not become an addict of anything. It will ruin your life. It's been ruining mine.

MY BEST FRIEND USED TO GO TO MY SCHOOL

BUT ENDED UP MOVING AWAY FOR A WHILE, AND WE WERE REALLY SAD ABOUT IT.

SHE WAS GONE FOR TWO YEARS UNTIL SHE MOVED BACK, AND WE WERE VERY EXCITED TO START GOING TO SCHOOL TOGETHER AGAIN.

THE FIRST COUPLE OF MONTHS WERE NORMAL EXCEPT EVERY GUY STARTED TO HAVE A CRUSH ON HER, AND SOME OF MY FRIENDS STARTED TO LIKE HER.

THIS MADE ME A BIT JEALOUS BECAUSE I DIDN'T GRAB GUYS' ATTENTION, AND SHE JUST DID IT SO EASILY. BUT I WAS FINE. IT WASN'T LIKE I WAS OVERWHELMED WITH JEALOUSY.

BUT THEN I STARTED TO NOTICE HOW SHE MADE ALL THESE NEW FRIENDS. IT WAS LIKE SHE JUST STARTED AT THE SCHOOL AND EVERYONE WANTED TO START TALKING TO HER AND BECOMING FRIENDS WITH HER.

11

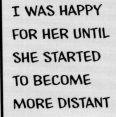

I WAS HAPPY FOR HER UNTIL SHE STARTED TO BECOME MORE DISTANT

AND WAY MORE IRRITABLE.

I'D ASK HER TO HANG OUT,

AND SHE'D ALWAYS SAY, "NO, I'M BUSY."

AND THEN I'D SEE HER ON SOCIAL MEDIA HANGING OUT WITH OTHER FRIENDS. AND I'D ASK HER, AND SHE'D JUST SAY, "PLANS JUST HAPPENED, I DIDN'T KNOW ABOUT IT."

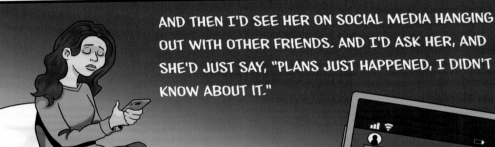

SHE SEEMED TO IGNORE ME AND NEVER ATTEMPTED TO TALK TO ME OR MAKE PLANS. SHE NEVER WENT OUT OF HER WAY TO SEE ME ANYMORE. I WAS TALKING TO SOME OTHER FRIENDS OF MINE, AND I LEARNED THAT SHE HAD JUST GROWN OUT OF ME.

IT REALLY HURT LEARNING SHE'D MOVED ON FROM ME, BUT HIGH SCHOOL JUST DOES THAT TO PEOPLE. YOU MAKE NEW FRIENDS, FALL INTO NEW GROUPS, BUT THE THING WAS, SHE BECAME FRIENDS WITH ALL OF MY OTHER FRIENDS AND I JUST GOT PUSHED OUT OF THAT GROUP.

I WAS LEFT ALONE.

WE'RE NOT BEST FRIENDS ANYMORE, AND IT REALLY HURTS. WE WERE BEST FRIENDS SINCE SECOND GRADE. I REALLY WANT OUR FRIENDSHIP TO GO BACK TO HOW IT WAS. THE JOKES, THE HANGING OUT, THE SLEEPOVERS. I MISS IT. BUT PEOPLE JUST CHANGE AND YOU GET PUSHED OUT, AND I WAS JUST ONE OF THOSE PEOPLE.

I turned from being bullied to a bully.

I was frie
with peop
who talke
me behind

I changed my entire personality just to fit in, and I'm not proud of myself for that.

My twin sister took my math test for me.

nds
le
d about
my back.

I'M SCARED TO THIS DAY TO TELL MY BEST FRIEND THAT I KISSED HER BOYFRIEND.

I WANT TO MAKE SCHOOL DISAPPEAR.

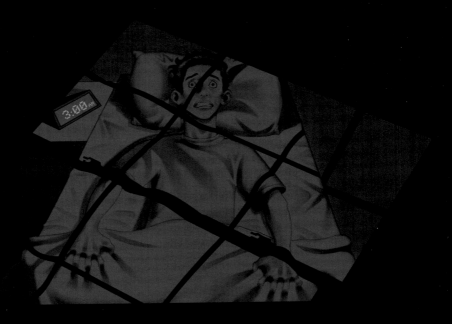

THE SUMMER BEFORE MY FIRST year of middle school I was really nervous about all the change to come. New school, new responsibilities, harder studies, classes changing, not being with my old friends. I was so nervous. I didn't want to go, but there was nothing I could do about it. I think this was a big part of what was to come.

It started with one sleepless night. I lay restless in my room until about 3:00 a.m. I just couldn't fall asleep. I couldn't sleep the following night or the night after that or the one after that. It got progressively worse. I started getting panic attacks.

It's like you can't breathe, like the breath is taken out of you.

I would start panting and breathing heavy. I wanted to stop, I really did, but I just couldn't. Sometimes I started sobbing, and I even lost feeling in some places like my arms or lips.

It was one of the scariest feelings I ever felt.

This began happening every night. It was so bad. I was thinking a whole bunch of other dark, scary thoughts. Sometimes I felt so strongly like something bad was going to happen if I fell asleep. Finally, it got so bad that I had to tell my parents what was really going on. At the time I couldn't name what was wrong. I knew what anxiety and panic attacks were, but I didn't think I could ever have them. Then with the help of my parents I realized what was happening and that I was having anxiety. It made me feel better to know what it was. I started middle school and realized it wasn't so bad. After that the anxiety began to slowly stop.

I still get anxiety sometimes about different things, especially at night, and it is still scary, but with my parents' help, I'm learning how to control it. If you're struggling with anxiety, you are not alone. You are not strange or weird for it. There is nothing wrong with you. You will be okay.

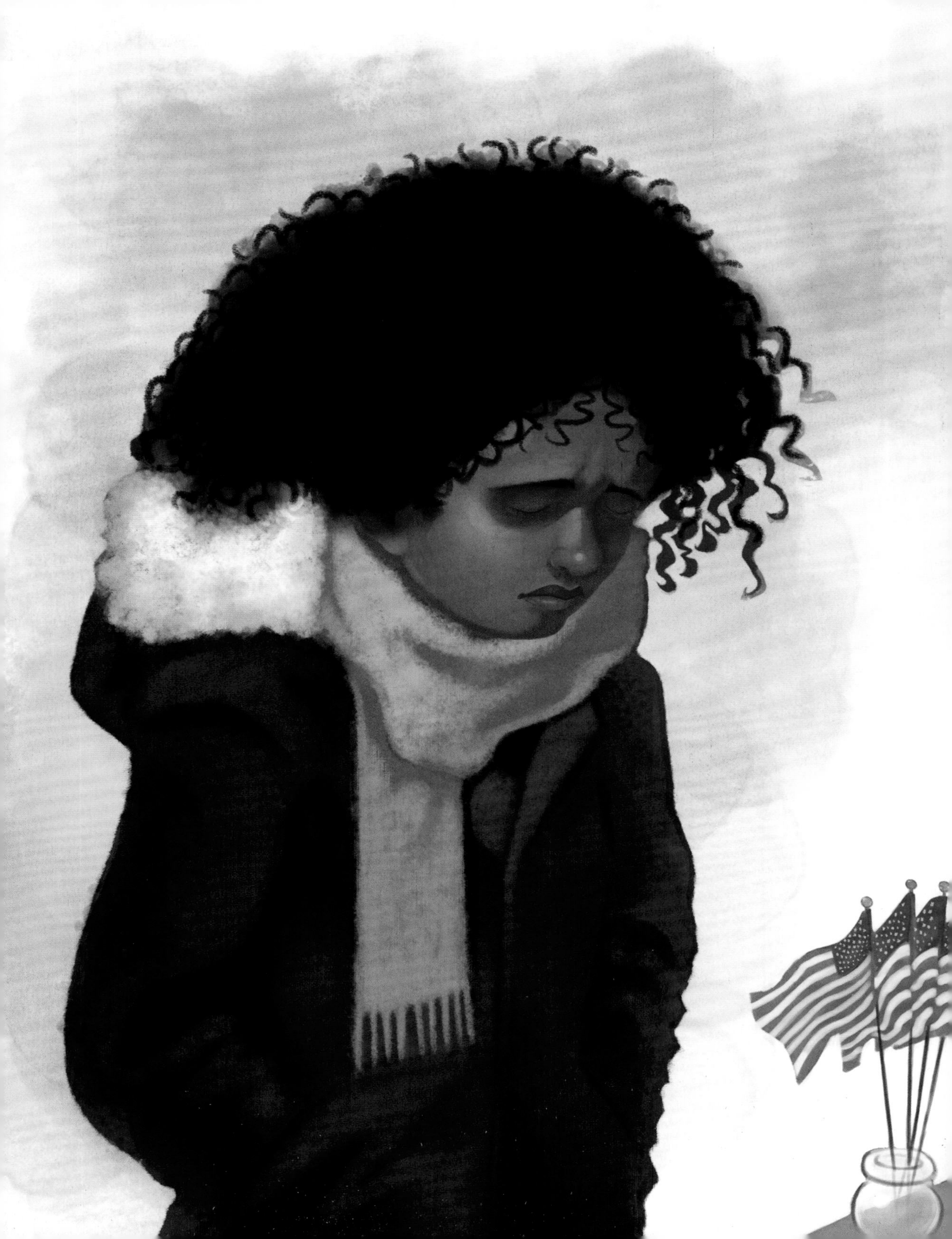

MY CLASS WENT TO WASHINGTON, DC, for a field trip. We were in a food court, and I was walking around looking for some of my friends since we'd all just gotten done with eating. I couldn't find them and figured they were in the gift shop. So I went to look for them, and I walked past this group of white boys. One of them looked over at me and said, "Guys, look how pretty she is." And the other one said, "Yeah, she is pretty, except the only problem is she's Black." When I heard that, my whole world just crumbled. I didn't under-stand why. Like, what did I do to deserve that? It just didn't make any sense to me.

19

I'M A TRANSGENDER BOY. THAT MEANS THAT I WAS BORN A GIRL BUT I AM A BOY.

I WANT TO USE THE BOYS' BATHROOM BUT I'M NOT ALLOWED, BECAUSE I GO TO A GIANT SCHOOL WITH A BUNCH OF HOMOPHOBES AND IT'S REALLY ANNOYING. MY PARENTS AREN'T PUTTING UP MUCH OF A FIGHT FOR THE BATHROOMS. THEY DON'T REALLY CARE; THEY DON'T REALLY UNDERSTAND IT ALL. SO THAT SUCKS.

THERE ARE THESE BATHROOMS RIGHT OUTSIDE THE SCHOOL BY THE FIELD, AND I HAD TO GO TO THE BATHROOM--I REALLY HAD TO GO.

NOBODY EVEN COUNTS THESE AS BATHROOMS ANYMORE. EVERYBODY THINKS THEY ARE JUST SPOOKY LITTLE ROOMS THAT HAPPEN TO HAVE A TOILET, SO I WENT INTO THE BOYS' BATHROOM.

A FEW PEOPLE SAW ME ENTER, AND THEY JUST THOUGHT I WAS A BIOLOGICAL BOY.
THEN THESE BOYS WALKED IN, AND THEY WERE LIKE,

WHAT ARE YOU DOING IN HERE?

THIS IS THE BOYS' BATHROOM!

I SLAMMED THE DOOR AND SAID,

HEY, I'M NOT DONE IN HERE! GET OUT!

I WAS HOPING THAT THEY DIDN'T SEE MY FACE. THEY STARTED SHOUTING AND SHOUTING,

THERE'S A GIRL IN THE BOYS' BATHROOM! THERE'S A GIRL IN THE BOYS' BATHROOM!

UGH. IT WAS HORRIBLE. I WAS SO EMBARRASSED. AND THE LOCK ON THE DOOR IN THE BATHROOM WAS BROKEN SO I HAD TO HOLD THE DOOR CLOSED, WHICH WAS REALLY DIFFICULT BECAUSE THERE WAS ONE OF ME AND TWO OF THEM.

A FEW OF MY FRIENDS CAME UP AND SAID,

OH SHUT UP. HE'S A BOY. HE CAN USE THAT BATHROOM, YOU IDIOTS.

AND THEY WERE LIKE,

NO, NO, NO. SHE'S A GIRL! BLAH, BLAH, BLAH, BLAH, BLAH.

AND ONE OF MY FRIENDS SAID,

LEAVE HIM ALONE! JUST LET HIM GO TO THE BATHROOM. HE'S A BOY, WHY DOES IT MATTER?

AND THEN THEY LAUGHED HORRIBLY HARD AND SAID,

'CAUSE HE'S NOT REALLY A BOY.

AND THAT JUST STUNG. EVENTUALLY MY FRIENDS GOT THE BOYS TO GO AWAY, AND I RAN OVER TO THE GIRLS' BATHROOM. I WAS JUST SOBBING AND IT WAS ALREADY LUNCHTIME SO I HAD TO GO TO LUNCH WITH RED EYEBALLS AND A RED FACE. IT WAS THE MOST EMBARRASSING EXPERIENCE OF MY LIFE.

ANYBODY OUT THERE WHO IS TRANSGENDER, YOU'RE WITH ME. AND IF YOU AREN'T, THEN JUST STAY SUPPORTIVE AND LOVE THOSE AROUND YOU.

IT takes

FEARL

DI

especially

WHEN YOU'R

ESSNESS

TO BE

FERENT

a teenager.

I made the dumbest mistake of my life. I

turned to him and asked,

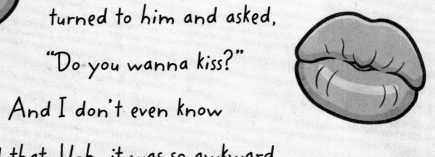

"Do you wanna kiss?"

And I don't even know

why I said that. Ugh, it was so awkward.

He was like sweating and shaking, didn't know what to

say. He was staring at me just speechless.

And I was just waiting, Oh no, oh no,

no, this is bad. This is just awful. Like,

that voice in my head

was like, No, just, just die. Just leave

and go home and die.

And he opened his mouth, and he said,

"You know, I don't really know you that well."

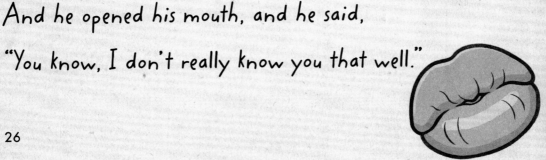

I was so embarrassed but also a little heartbroken,

because I really, really wanted to kiss him.

I STARTED AT A NEW school and all of a sudden everything was really hard. I went from knowing exactly what I was doing all the time to feeling totally lost and alone. My classes were remote because of the COVID pandemic and suddenly more challenging than ever. I wasn't sure I even understood what the teacher was asking for a lot of the time. I got really upset. And I, like, just stopped trying. I hid under my covers. I didn't log on to class when I was supposed to. I didn't turn in my homework. My mom would ask, "Why does your hair look so greasy? Why don't you take a shower?" I would just shrug.

Then my teachers started sending notes home about how I wasn't participating in class. My mom got them and asked why I wasn't logging on or doing my homework. I told her how lost I felt. She asked me why I didn't ask for help. I told her I didn't think I was supposed to. I felt like I was supposed to handle it all on my own—and if I couldn't, well, that was my problem.

Then a thing happened that I didn't expect. My mom didn't yell or punish me. She hugged me. She told me that she was always here to help me and that I should always ask for her help when I needed it. She said that was her job, and helping me was all she wanted to do.

She also said that hiding under my covers wasn't going to make my problems go away. It was only going to make them bigger.

AROUND TEN YEARS AGO, MY mom walked into my bedroom to tell me something that would change both of our lives forever. "I met another man, and we're going to get married," she told me. I was shocked, angry, and sad, all at once. How could she leave my dad? How could he let her? And who was this new man? Why was she crying when she did this to our family? Even though my mom explained that she had to follow her heart, the strong, conflicting emotions I had inside me wouldn't go away. I was worried about my dad and how he was going to deal with this. He's always needed my mom. They were a team, and we were meant to be a family. But now, ten years later, my mom and dad are both remarried. I learned so much more from my new parents than just from my own. My life has been filled with more love than I thought possible. My parents' experience has taught me many things. Like even bad experiences have the potential to lead to good ones.

MY BROTHER HAS BEEN PLAYING FOOTBALL SINCE HE WAS SIX YEARS OLD. AND WHEN I WAS YOUNGER I ACTUALLY HAD A LOT OF FUN WATCHING HIM PLAYING AND HANGING OUT WITH MY FRIENDS AT THE FOOTBALL FIELD.

BUT OUR LIFE IS DIFFERENT AT HOME THAN IT IS AT THE FOOTBALL STADIUM. AT THE STADIUM I'M HIS PROUD BIG SISTER, SUPPORTING HIM AT EVERY GAME. BUT AT HOME, I'M JEALOUS OF HIM. I FEEL LIKE I'M CONSTANTLY COMPETING FOR OUR PARENTS' ATTENTION.

JUST BECAUSE HE PLAYS FOOTBALL IT FEELS LIKE IT'S ALL ABOUT HIM--ALL ABOUT FOOTBALL PRACTICE AND THE NEXT GAME. IT FEELS LIKE THEY'RE CONSTANTLY PRAISING HIM.

THEY'RE ALWAYS TALKING ABOUT HOW HE'S SUCH A GREAT FOOTBALL PLAYER AND HE DOES THIS AND HE DOES THAT--IT'S ALL ABOUT HIM AND NOTHING ABOUT ME.

I CAN'T TELL YOU HOW MANY TIMES I'VE HAD A MELTDOWN BECAUSE I FEEL LIKE I SHOULDN'T HAVE TO COMPETE WITH MY BROTHER TO GET ATTENTION FROM OUR PARENTS.

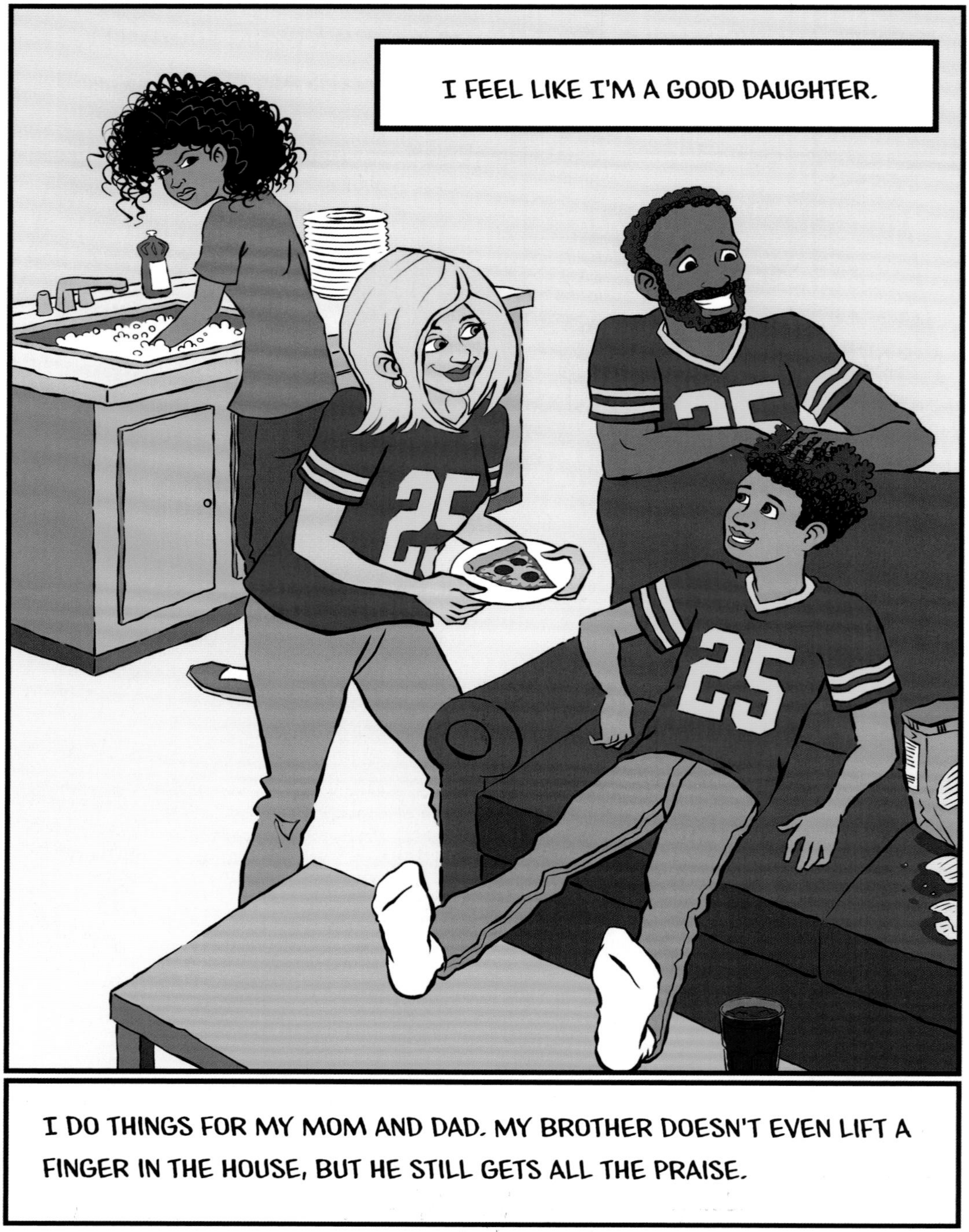
I FEEL LIKE I'M A GOOD DAUGHTER.
I DO THINGS FOR MY MOM AND DAD. MY BROTHER DOESN'T EVEN LIFT A FINGER IN THE HOUSE, BUT HE STILL GETS ALL THE PRAISE.

JUST TODAY I LOOKED AT MY MOM'S INSTAGRAM--SHE HAS NOT POSTED ONE PICTURE OF ME OR FOR ME IN OVER A YEAR-- IT'S ALL ABOUT MY BROTHER.

IT MAKES ME FEEL VERY INADEQUATE, AND I SHOULDN'T FEEL LIKE THAT. I'M THEIR DAUGHTER. I SHOULD FEEL EQUALLY PRAISED AND HAPPY. WELL, I'M NOT. IT'S STILL NOT BETTER, BUT WHAT CAN I DO?

EVER SINCE I WAS LITTLE, I'VE ALWAYS BEEN SCARED OF MY MOM.

I try my

to make

happy b

make my

My crush told me
I'm a bad kisser.

I had a terrible teacher. He kind of ruined our childhood a lot by saying the Easter bunny, the tooth fairy, and stuff does not exist.

I'm depressed and nobody believes me.

best others t I can't self.

I REGRET NOT SEEING MY GRANDPA BEFORE HE DIED.

ONE NIGHT I GOT A notification saying that I'd been added to a group chat. I clicked on the notification, but I was immediately removed. The next afternoon the notification was still there. I clicked on it again and this time I could see what the whole group chat was saying.

Basically, people in my year had a secret group chat dedicated to me.

As I scrolled, the topic turned to how I apparently was morally opposed to wearing bras and all sorts of rumors that I didn't know about. I was thinking, you know, "This isn't so bad. I've experienced worse." But the more I scrolled, the worse it got. They were taking pictures and screenshots of things from my Instagram and posting them in the chat. They took one of the pictures of my friends and posted racist remarks, saying how they all smell bad and that they

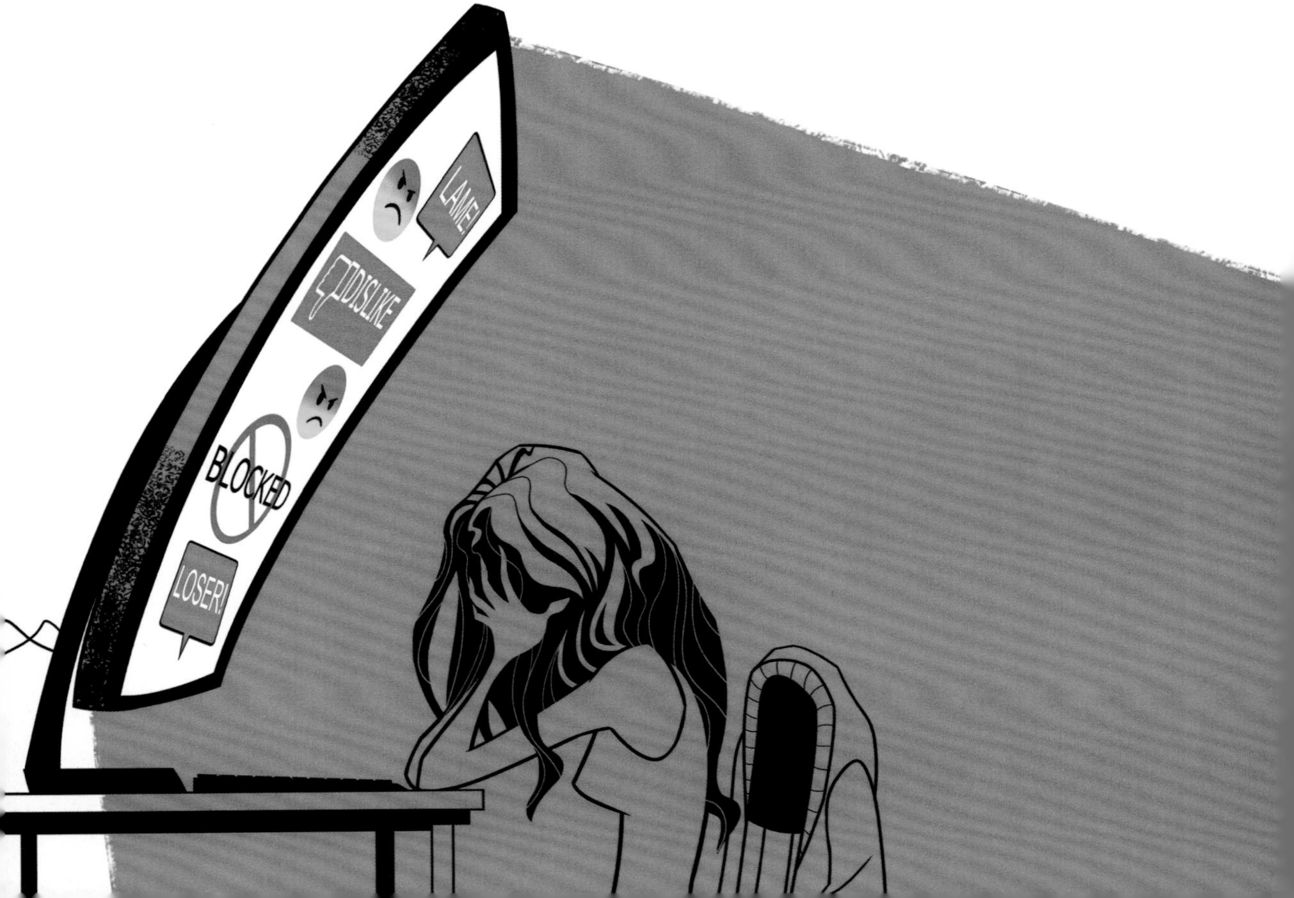
LAME!
DISLIKE
BLOCKED
LOSER!

were dirty because of being friends with me. They also went onto my dad's profile and took a picture of me on a bouncy castle, saying that I was trying to be sexy and making remarks about my body, especially my breasts. A boy entered the chat and claimed he couldn't stand being in the same classes as me, because apparently I smelled awful, and he also posted pornographic images and claimed they were of me.

I burst into tears and felt worse than I ever felt in my whole life. I phoned my friends and told them everything and finally managed to report these people to the head teacher and showed them the screenshots of the chat I had taken. However, I didn't get the justice I deserved because nothing happened to these people, and I really wish it had.

I STARTED TO DELIBERATELY ALTER my style and tried to make myself look like the popular girls. All I wanted was to look just like everyone else. Deep down I loved my traditional Pakistani clothing, but looking back, my desperation for popularity was stopping me from loving who I really was. Crop tops, ripped jeans, and T-shirts. Everyone seemed to be happy wearing those. Not me. I was comfortable in a kameez and my hijab. It took time for me to embrace my culture in public, but in the end, it was definitely worth it to feel happy.

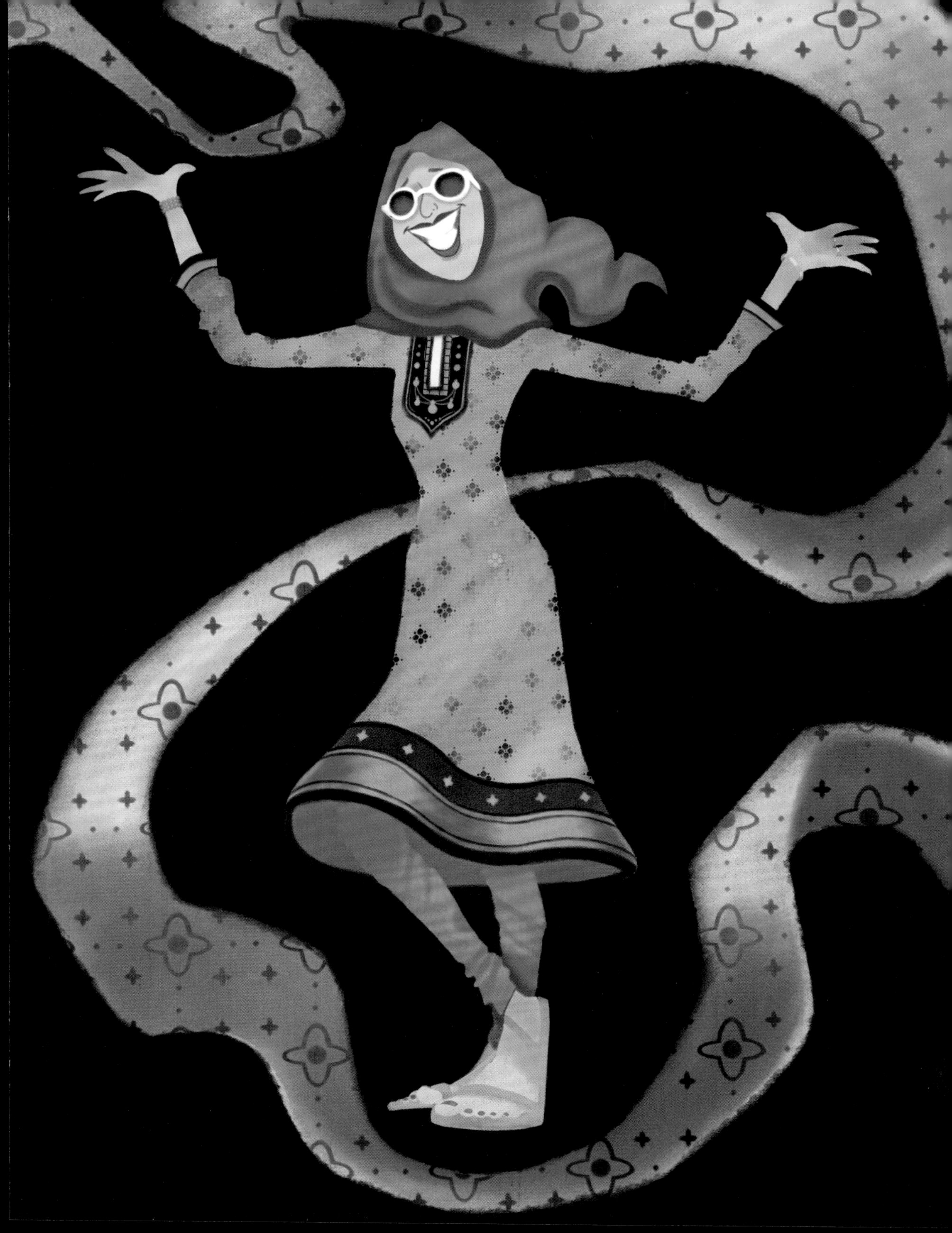

WHEN THE DAY OF THE final exam came around I wasn't looking forward to it. I'd studied the night before, but as stressed out as I was, all the stuff that I had studied for, all the knowledge that was in my head, disappeared.

I didn't know what to do. My mind was just so blank. When the test started, the teacher handed it out saying, "No phones, no cheating, blah, blah, blah, blah, blah." My mind just started telling me, *Oh, you're gonna fail this. You might as well just get up and walk out of this class right now. Consider yourself a failure. Go to summer school.*

So I cheated. I regret it, but I did.

I WORE HATS ALL THE time to cover my acne and avoided talking to people because of how ashamed and embarrassed I was. I had a group of friends that I hung out with, and all of them had clear and glowing skin and it only brought my self-esteem down.

SINCE I WAS LITTLE, I always tried to be perfect for other people. I looked for their approval. I thought I had to be perfect to be included. So what I did was compare myself to those I thought were perfect and punish myself if I wasn't like them. These punishments went from saying stuff to myself like *You're so stupid* to pinching or hitting myself. I was immersed in this world where if I wasn't perfect, then I wasn't worth anything, and in the end I kinda lost the real me.

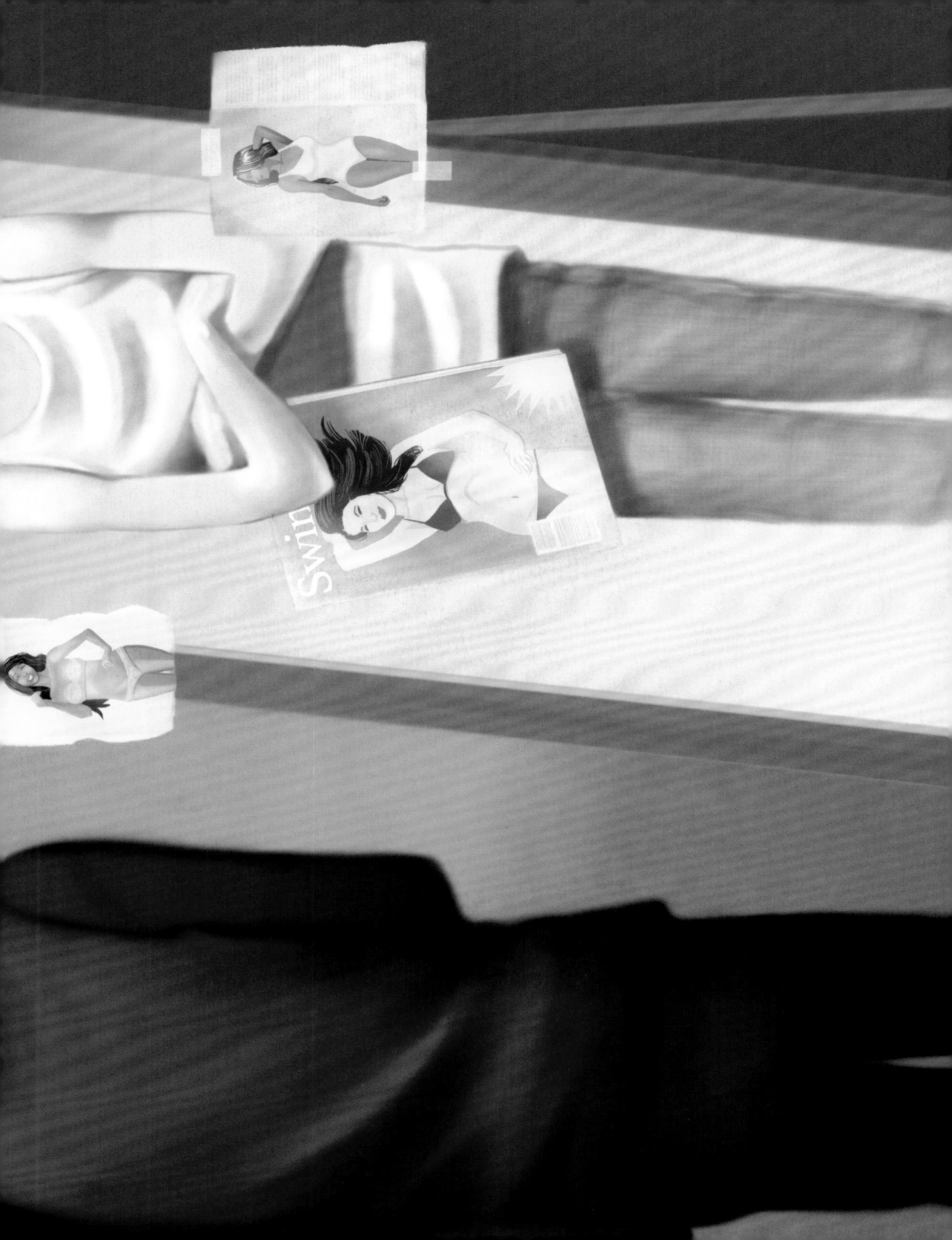

NEVER G

THE PERSON

HOLE —

it's A LO

all DOWN

AL DEGRADING

ONG WAY UP.

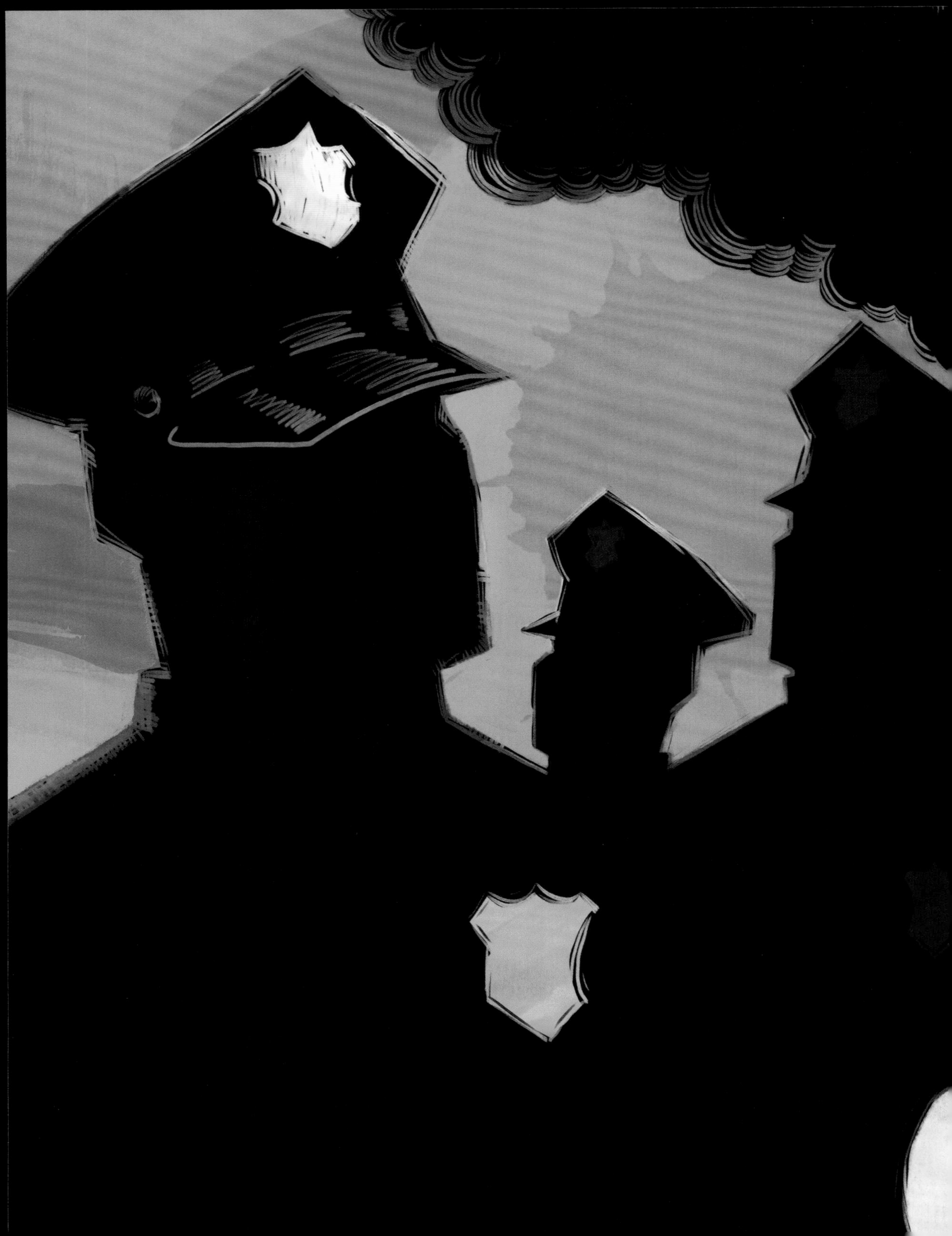

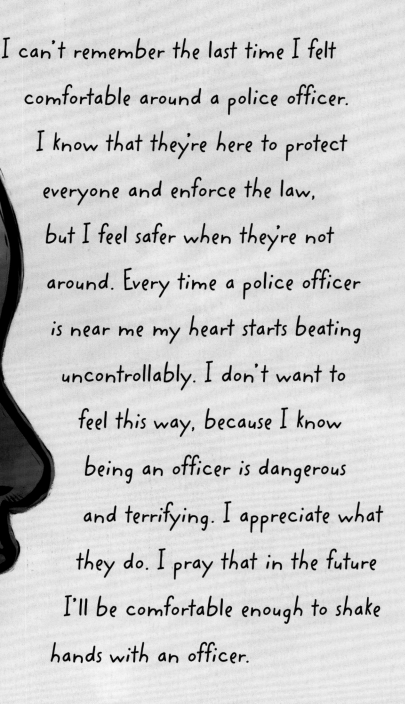

I can't remember the last time I felt
comfortable around a police officer.
I know that they're here to protect
everyone and enforce the law,
but I feel safer when they're not
around. Every time a police officer
is near me my heart starts beating
uncontrollably. I don't want to
feel this way, because I know
being an officer is dangerous
and terrifying. I appreciate what
they do. I pray that in the future
I'll be comfortable enough to shake
hands with an officer.

I HAVE ADHD. BASICALLY, I'M always full of energy. I can never sit down and stay in one spot. Sitting down in a chair for six hours is really hard for me. Having ADHD also feels like having two minds—both minds can think whatever they want, and they both can focus on two different things at once.

It's impossible to concentrate on what the teachers are saying when my mind is having an even more, well, interesting discussion.

And even a little thing like a bird flying outside will distract me completely.

One day in language arts my teacher gave us some instructions. She told us to go and read some chapters of a book. So while my ADHD was taking over, I missed some parts of her instructions. I read three chapters of the book and then started to doodle in my notebook. The teacher walked over to my desk

and grabbed my notebook. She started flipping through it. When she got to the page where I was supposed to write down quotes from the book, she straight-up shamed me in front of the class. She brought me to the front of the classroom and said, "Don't act like him. He didn't follow my instructions." It was so embarrassing.

She took me outside the classroom and asked me why the frick I didn't listen. So I explained to her that I have ADHD, what it's like, and that it's hard for me to focus. I sincerely apologized for it. And she just called me a liar.

So my teacher gave me a new seat right in front of her desk, and she looks at me all the time. And, I mean, it just seems unfair. I've always wanted to tell somebody about it, but I haven't.

And so I just wanted to tell you guys: if you are struggling, if your teacher is making fun of you like mine did, if your teacher is not understanding—you should go tell someone. Don't be like me, guys. Don't wait.

SO MY BEST FRIEND AND I WERE SITTING IN CLASS, AND WE WERE JUST WAITING FOR OUR NEW HISTORY TEACHER BECAUSE OUR LAST HISTORY TEACHER GOT PREGNANT. THEN THE DOOR OPENED AND THIS GUY WALKED IN AND SAID HE WAS GONNA BE OUR NEW HISTORY TEACHER.

50

OUR MOUTHS WERE LITERALLY OPEN, AND WE COULDN'T EVEN TALK BECAUSE HE WAS SO CUTE. YOU COULD SEE HIS MUSCLES, HIS ABS THROUGH HIS T-SHIRT, AND WE WERE JUST GIGGLING TALKING ABOUT HIM. THEN IN THE MIDDLE OF CLASS HE SAID WE SHOULD SHUT UP BECAUSE WE WERE REALLY LOUD.

WE REALLY WANTED TO CONTINUE TALKING ABOUT HIM BECAUSE THIS WAS SO OVERWHELMING, SO I STARTED WRITING A NOTE THAT I WAS GONNA PASS TO MY FRIEND. BUT THE TEACHER SAW ME WRITING THIS LETTER, AND HE TOOK IT OUT OF MY HAND AND DECIDED TO READ IT IN FRONT OF THE WHOLE CLASS. I SAID,

NO, NO, NO, NO, DON'T READ THAT. THIS IS SUPER PRIVATE!

AND HE SAID,

NO. I INSIST.

I WAS LIKE,
OH MY GOD, YEAH, OKAY.
THIS IS THE END. BYE-BYE.

AND HE STARTED READING IT OUT LOUD FOR THE WHOLE CLASS TO HEAR. HE READ, "DON'T YOU THINK THE NEW HISTORY TEACHER IS SO FREAKING HOT? OH MY GOD. I WANT TO MARRY THIS GUY." HE TURNED BRIGHT RED. I TURNED BRIGHT RED.

THE WHOLE CLASS WAS LAUGHING, AND HE SAID, "UM, YEAH, UM, I'M--I'M SORRY ABOUT THAT." AND I WAS THINKING, **OH MY GOD. PLEASE, I JUST WANNA DIE.**

I put on a mask that everything was fine on the outside, but on the inside I was broken to pieces.

My crus
me ugly
of every

I shoplifted a fish, successfully.
I named him Gilbert.

I've been used too
many times in my life,
not gonna lie.

called
in front
one.

MY TWO BEST FRIENDS
DITCHED ME
AFTER HIGH SCHOOL.

Having ADHD and Asperger's
is hard for me. We aren't weirdos.
We just do things differently.

I HAD THIS FRIEND. She was pretty nice at first. She was really funny. I'd do a lot of fun things with her, and she was just always sort of there for me whenever I needed her. But as time went on, a darker side of her began to emerge. She'd insult me, bully me, make fun of me, and try to embarrass me in public sometimes. She'd call me names, like fat, ugly, stupid, and a lot of other things that typical bullies say.

As time went on, she kept bullying and insulting me. I didn't really want to do anything, because I thought that if I stood up to her, she'd only get angrier at me and she'd bully me even more. Eventually she crossed a line when she called me a really offensive word over text that I prefer not to say. At that point I kind of realized,

WOW, MAYBE I SHOULDN'T LET HER BULLY ME LIKE THIS. MAYBE I SHOULD TALK BACK TO HER.

And that's what I did. I confronted her at school the next day. I said to her, "You cannot keep doing this to me. You cannot keep bullying me and insulting me. I think this friendship is just over." I just walked away and sort of ended things with her. I stopped hanging out with her, and I eventually learned to befriend nicer people who actually cared about me and who complimented me instead of bullying me.

I'm glad that I ended our friendship, because if somebody is constantly making me feel bad about myself, then I don't have time for that person. Although sometimes I do miss her, because I did actually have some fun times with her. But then I remind myself that she was a bully, not a friend. She was making me feel bad about myself. And that's why I shouldn't have been friends with her.

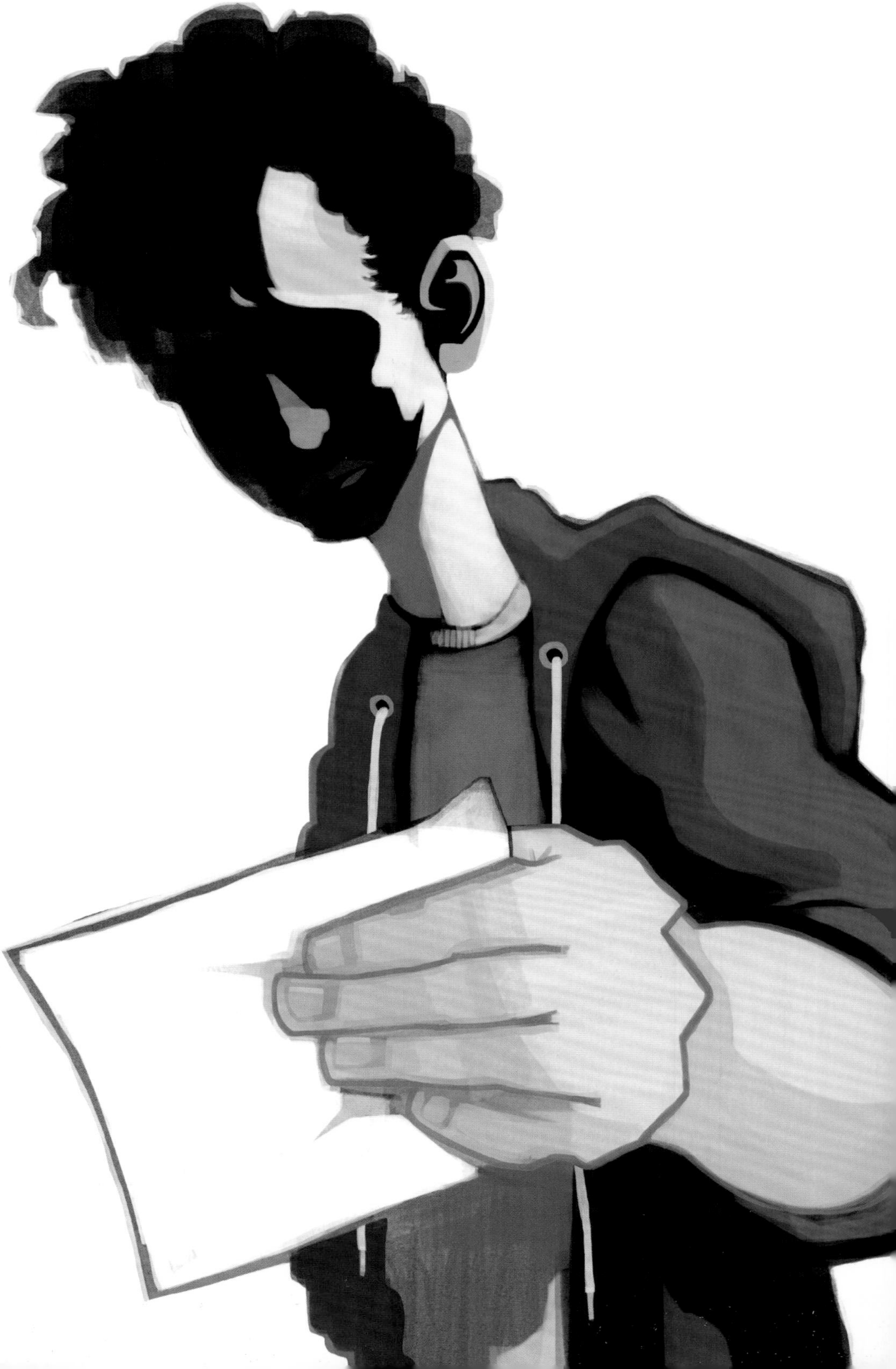

I was a Jew living in a Christian-dominated town. I was prepping for social studies, and in the middle of class I felt a rustle in my hoodie, so I checked my hood. There was a flash card in there with a drawing of an anti-Semitic symbol with the word "heil" around it. On the other side, it was a degrading racial term I'd rather not say. Reading a note like that is like having a mental slap in the face. I get anti-Semitic slurs thrown at me all the time, and some of these people are supposed to be my best friends.

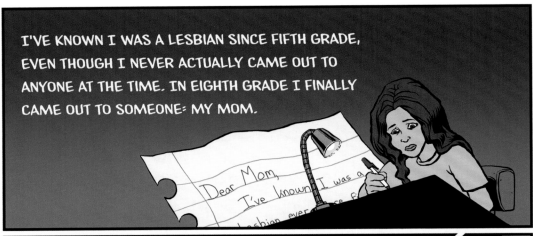

I'VE KNOWN I WAS A LESBIAN SINCE FIFTH GRADE, EVEN THOUGH I NEVER ACTUALLY CAME OUT TO ANYONE AT THE TIME. IN EIGHTH GRADE I FINALLY CAME OUT TO SOMEONE: MY MOM.

I WAS TOO NERVOUS TO MEET HER FACE-TO-FACE, SO I WROTE HER A NOTE TALKING ABOUT HOW I WAS A LESBIAN AND LEFT IT ON HER BED.
BUT I DIDN'T GET AN ANSWER IN RETURN.

THE NEXT DAY, THOUGH, I HEARD HER TALKING ABOUT ME ON THE PHONE TO HER BEST FRIEND.

SHE SAID, "IT'S JUST A PHASE, RIGHT? I DON'T HAVE A GAY DAUGHTER."
ALL THROUGH THAT WEEK I WAS A NERVOUS WRECK, THINKING,

I'M DISGUSTING. HOW COULD I EVEN SAY THAT TO HER? MOM'S GOING TO DISOWN ME.

SHE NEVER SAID ANYTHING ABOUT IT. SHE JUST WENT ON LIKE NOTHING HAD HAPPENED.

I'VE BEEN STRUGGLING WITH DEPRESSION for a couple of years. I'd get sad for no reason. I wouldn't want to get out of bed in the mornings, and I wouldn't want to go to school. I couldn't deal with my own problems, and I couldn't stand the thought of waking up every day and having the same thing happen over and over again.

So I went to my parents' bathroom and I took a bottle of pills—I took twenty-two of them. It was nighttime medicine, so I started getting very drowsy and then I remember feeling the need to throw up. I saw my brother was in the bathroom, and I had nowhere else to go so I just threw up on the carpet right in the hall. My parents came out of their room very confused, and I told them what I'd done. They started to freak out, and my dad took me to the ER.

I was in the hospital for three days. After they made sure I was physically healthy, they had to make sure I was mentally healthy. So I went to a mental hospital, where I got to meet some other people there with similar stories. And it felt kind of good to know that you're not alone.

I slowly started recovering. However, with the thing I did, it was a huge deal, so I had to see a psychiatrist. He diagnosed me with a depressive disorder and I have to take anti-depressants.

I've been at home for about a month now, and things are getting better. I see my therapist regularly, and we are confronting my feelings. Things are looking up.

SOMET
BEING
heali

IMES
SAD IS A
i'ng PROCESS

WE SHOULDN'T HAVE DONE IT. WE WERE SO STUPID. BUT AFTER BEING IN QUARANTINE AND NOT SEEING EACH OTHER FOR MONTHS, MY FRIENDS AND I STARTED TO GO STIR-CRAZY.

WE WERE ALL LEAVING FOR COLLEGE IN A MONTH AND WANTED TO SEE EACH OTHER BEFORE WE LEFT. SO, IN THE MIDDLE OF A NATIONAL PANDEMIC THAT HAD TAKEN THE LIVES OF MILLIONS, WE PLANNED A PARTY. THIRTY OF US CROWDED INTO A BASEMENT AND DID EVERYTHING BUT SOCIAL DISTANCE. I THOUGHT WE WERE INVINCIBLE.

I DIDN'T THINK IT COULD HAPPEN TO US. BUT A FEW DAYS AFTER OUR STUPID PARTY, WE FOUND OUT THAT ONE OF OUR FRIENDS FROM THE PARTY TESTED POSITIVE FOR COVID-19.

WE IMMEDIATELY FREAKED OUT AND SELF-QUARANTINED.
UNFORTUNATELY, THE DAMAGE WAS DONE. AT 2:00 A.M. ON
MY SECOND DAY OF QUARANTINE, MY FRIEND TEXTED IN A GROUP
CHAT THAT SHE HAD A FEVER. MINUTES LATER, TEXTS CAME
FLOODING IN FROM MY OTHER FRIENDS THAT THEY TOO HAD
DEVELOPED FEVERS.

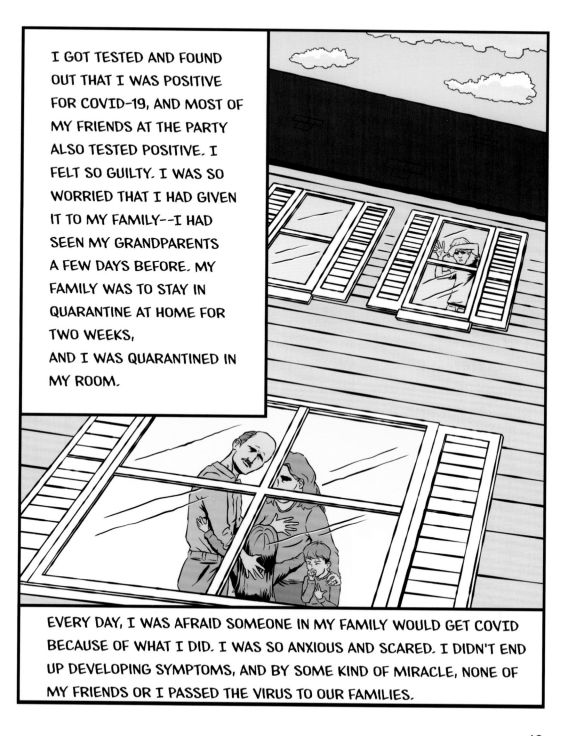

I GOT TESTED AND FOUND OUT THAT I WAS POSITIVE FOR COVID-19, AND MOST OF MY FRIENDS AT THE PARTY ALSO TESTED POSITIVE. I FELT SO GUILTY. I WAS SO WORRIED THAT I HAD GIVEN IT TO MY FAMILY--I HAD SEEN MY GRANDPARENTS A FEW DAYS BEFORE. MY FAMILY WAS TO STAY IN QUARANTINE AT HOME FOR TWO WEEKS, AND I WAS QUARANTINED IN MY ROOM.

EVERY DAY, I WAS AFRAID SOMEONE IN MY FAMILY WOULD GET COVID BECAUSE OF WHAT I DID. I WAS SO ANXIOUS AND SCARED. I DIDN'T END UP DEVELOPING SYMPTOMS, AND BY SOME KIND OF MIRACLE, NONE OF MY FRIENDS OR I PASSED THE VIRUS TO OUR FAMILIES.

WHEN MY MOM TESTED NEGATIVE TWO WEEKS LATER, SHE CRIED, AND I REALIZED HOW SCARED SHE MUST HAVE BEEN WHILE OUR FAMILY WAS IN QUARANTINE WAITING TO SEE IF WE WOULD DEVELOP SYMPTOMS. THIS WAS A WAKE-UP CALL FOR ME.

I BEAT MYSELF UP FOR MONTHS AFTER GOING TO THE PARTY, BUT I'M GLAD THAT IT TAUGHT ME A VALUABLE LESSON ABOUT BEING CONSIDERATE OF OTHERS, AND REALIZING THAT I AM NOT, IN FACT, INVINCIBLE. I HAVE JUST AS MUCH A ROLE IN KEEPING PEOPLE SAFE AS EVERYONE ELSE DURING COVID.

KIDS STARTED MAKING FUN OF me because everyone started developing and I didn't. All my friends did, but they had really big curves, and standing next to them just made me look like I was a frickin' cereal box.

WE HAVE SO LITTLE BREAK time at school. Whenever I try to buy lunch, the bell rings and I have to go to my next class without having eaten. They give so much homework every day. I arrive home at four thirty and spend the rest of the hours doing my homework. The homework is so frickin' a lot that I will go to sleep at eleven and wake up at three in the morning to continue with homework until it's done.

ME, MY MOM, AND MY BROTHER HAVE ALWAYS MOVED AROUND THE CITY BECAUSE WE WEREN'T FINANCIALLY STABLE. MY MOM WAS LOW INCOME, WHICH MEANS WE WERE NOT RICH. WE WERE POOR. WE NEVER REALLY HAD ANYTHING, BUT WE HAD CLOTHES ON OUR BACKS AND FOOD IN OUR STOMACHS AND THAT'S ALL THAT MATTERED.

WE STARTED SCHOOL IN THE BRONX. MY BROTHER MADE FRIENDS THERE. MY MOM THOUGHT HIS NEW FRIENDS WERE LOVELY PEOPLE, BUT THEY WEREN'T. THEY WERE BAD. THEY WERE ALL INTO DRUGS.

MY BROTHER STARTED HANGING OUT WITH THEM MORE THAN HE DID WITH ME AND MY MOM, AND HE STARTED MAKING A BUNCH OF MONEY. MY MOM DIDN'T REALLY THINK MUCH OF IT.

HE JUST SAID HE WAS WORKING OVERTIME . . .

WHICH I KNEW WAS A LIE.

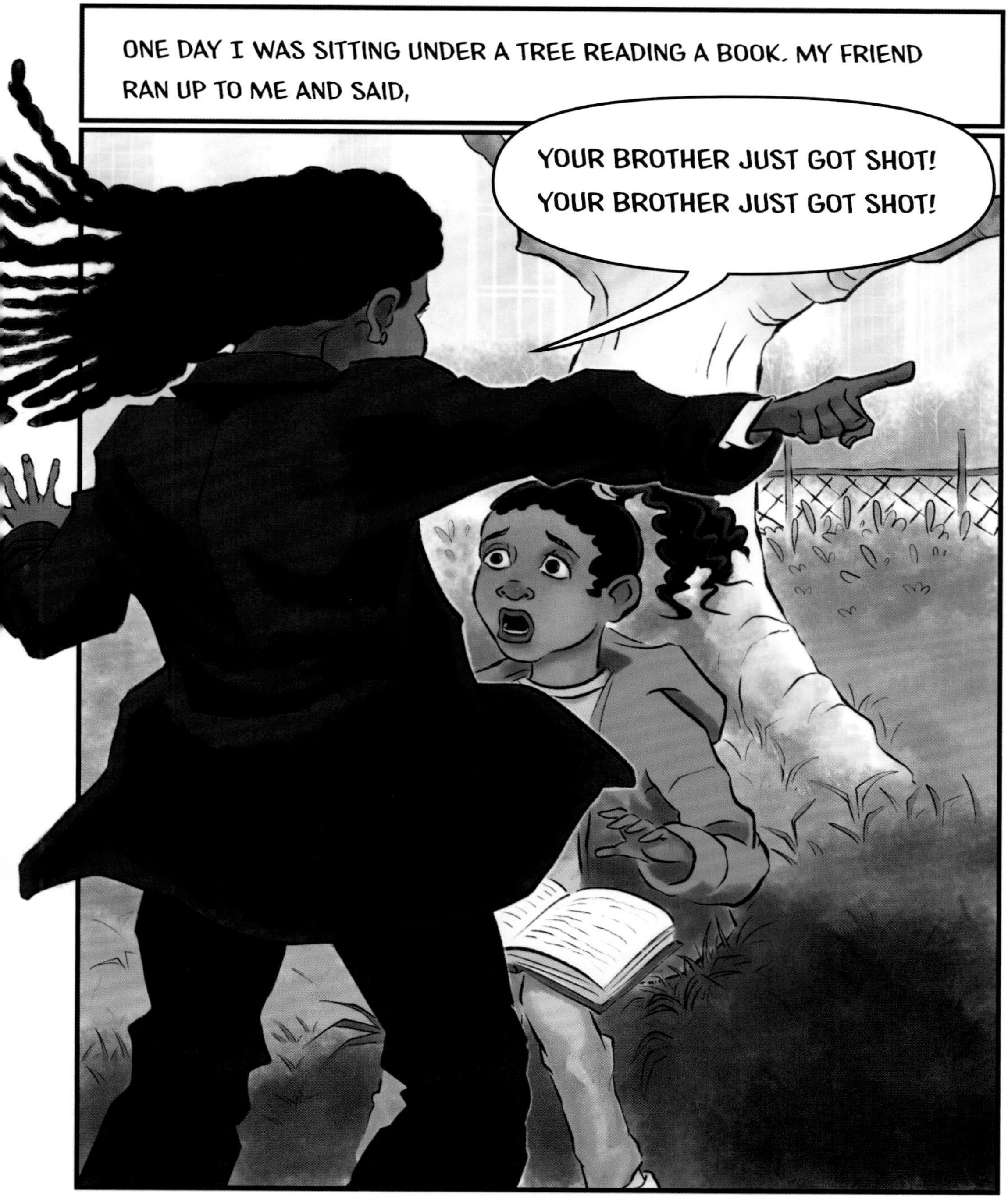
ONE DAY I WAS SITTING UNDER A TREE READING A BOOK. MY FRIEND RAN UP TO ME AND SAID,
YOUR BROTHER JUST GOT SHOT! YOUR BROTHER JUST GOT SHOT!

I RAN AND FOLLOWED HER. THERE HE WAS, LYING IN A POOL OF BLOOD. I JUST STOOD THERE. I COULDN'T MOVE. MY EARS STARTED TO RING. I DIDN'T KNOW WHAT WAS HAPPENING. I WAS IN SHOCK. SOMEBODY CALLED AN AMBULANCE, BUT IT WAS TOO LATE. MY BROTHER WAS ALREADY GONE.

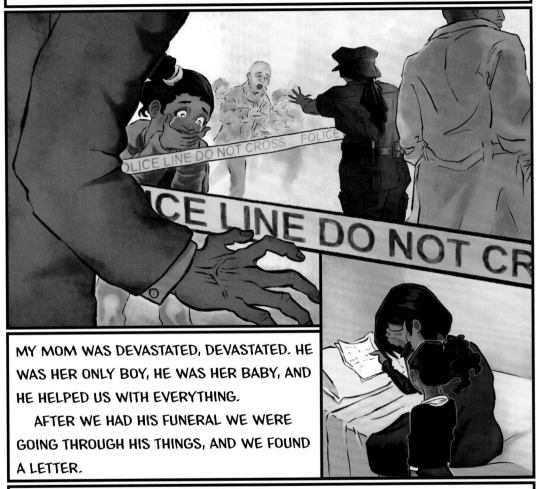

MY MOM WAS DEVASTATED, DEVASTATED. HE WAS HER ONLY BOY, HE WAS HER BABY, AND HE HELPED US WITH EVERYTHING.

AFTER WE HAD HIS FUNERAL WE WERE GOING THROUGH HIS THINGS, AND WE FOUND A LETTER.

IT SAID, "IF YOU'RE READING THIS, I'M ALREADY DEAD." IT TOLD MY MOM THE TRUTH ABOUT WHERE HE WAS GETTING THE MONEY. IT SAID THAT HE WAS DRUG DEALING, HE WAS GETTING IN WITH THE WRONG PEOPLE. HE WAS SELLING DRUGS SO WE COULD HAVE WHAT WE WANTED.

"HE WASN'T SUPPOSED TO DO THAT," MY MOM CRIED. "HE WAS SUPPOSED TO BE THE KID, AND I WAS SUPPOSED TO BE THE PARENT AND TAKE CARE OF HIM."

HE'S GONE. IT STILL HURTS TO TALK ABOUT IT, BUT THERE'S NOTHING I CAN DO NOW.

I love anime and all the popular girls think I'm a ~~freak~~ because of it.

I'm at the ~~of my clas~~ ~~of my gra~~ I'm miser

MY PARENTS ALWAYS FIGHT.

When you're getting teased and bullied, everybody thinks that you're fine. You don't have feelings or you don't care but little do they know that you go home and cry all night.

top

s because

des but

ble.

I farted
in front of my crush.

Everyone needs somewhere to sit at lunch. If you don't have somewhere to sit at lunch, it changes everything.

Last year I was over at my friend's house, and we started to have a conversation about love. I asked her, "Do you have a crush on anyone?" And she said, "I had a crush on this boy, and I recently broke up with my girlfriend." I said, "You're kidding me, right? You're gay?" She's like, "I'm bi." I was in shock. I'm a Roman Catholic, and I'm a little bit homophobic. I don't really like gay people that much. I don't like bisexual people either.

So I'm just trying to breathe. I went home, and I was in shock. I couldn't sleep that night, just thinking about how she's bi and stuff. The next day I woke up and thought to myself, Okay. She's my friend. She's been by my side for a really long time, and I shouldn't judge her by her sexuality. There's nothing wrong with being bisexual. So I went over to her house, and she said, "Are you okay with me being bi? I know it might be weird." And I said, "Yeah, I'm fine with it. You're my best friend. I don't really care about your sexuality."

MY HOMOPHOBIA WENT AWAY, AND I DON'T THINK THAT GAY PEOPLE ARE BAD ANYMORE.

So, if you're homophobic, just please don't be. You shouldn't judge anyone by what their sexuality is.

I HATED MYSELF SO MUCH because our teachers used to tell us that being gay and Muslim can harm you a lot, can make you a bad person, a horrible person, and can get you into hell. I used to tell myself, "Oh my God. I'm a horrible person for being, for being me." I tried to change who I was, but I just couldn't. I just couldn't.

I HAD THIS GIRLFRIEND. WHEN we first met, it was like love at first sight. I just loved her so much.

One day I'm on Instagram and I'm just scrolling. I noticed that my girlfriend unfollowed me. Both of our accounts are private—I follow her, she follows me, so it was weird. I texted her and asked why she did that. And she said she didn't realize and must have done it by accident.

But rumors started to spread that she was flirting with another guy and that she was getting together with him. I decided to approach her and ask if it was true. At first she threw a book of excuses at me, but eventually she just admitted it and screamed, "I don't like you anymore!" I just felt betrayed. I was so angry, because I did everything for her and didn't understand why she did this. It was very depressing at the time.

But eventually you've just got to learn to get over things, because life can be like that.

I WISH I COULD GO back to the past and save myself from joining a gang.

WHEN I WAS IN MIDDLE school, I got bullied really bad. People just picked on me. And it stayed like that for about three years. I was bullied mercilessly. I was called names, stuff got thrown at me, and people would write mean names on the bathroom walls and call me horrible stuff. It got to the point where it got physical. I was actually beaten up by multiple people just walking down the hallway for literally no reason.

My parents did everything that they could do, but the principals and teachers just didn't seem to care enough. Nothing ever really got done to stop it. It was a terrible time for me, tragic and traumatizing. And I was scared. I hated going to school. I didn't wanna be there. I was depressed and afraid. It was very stressful and difficult for me.

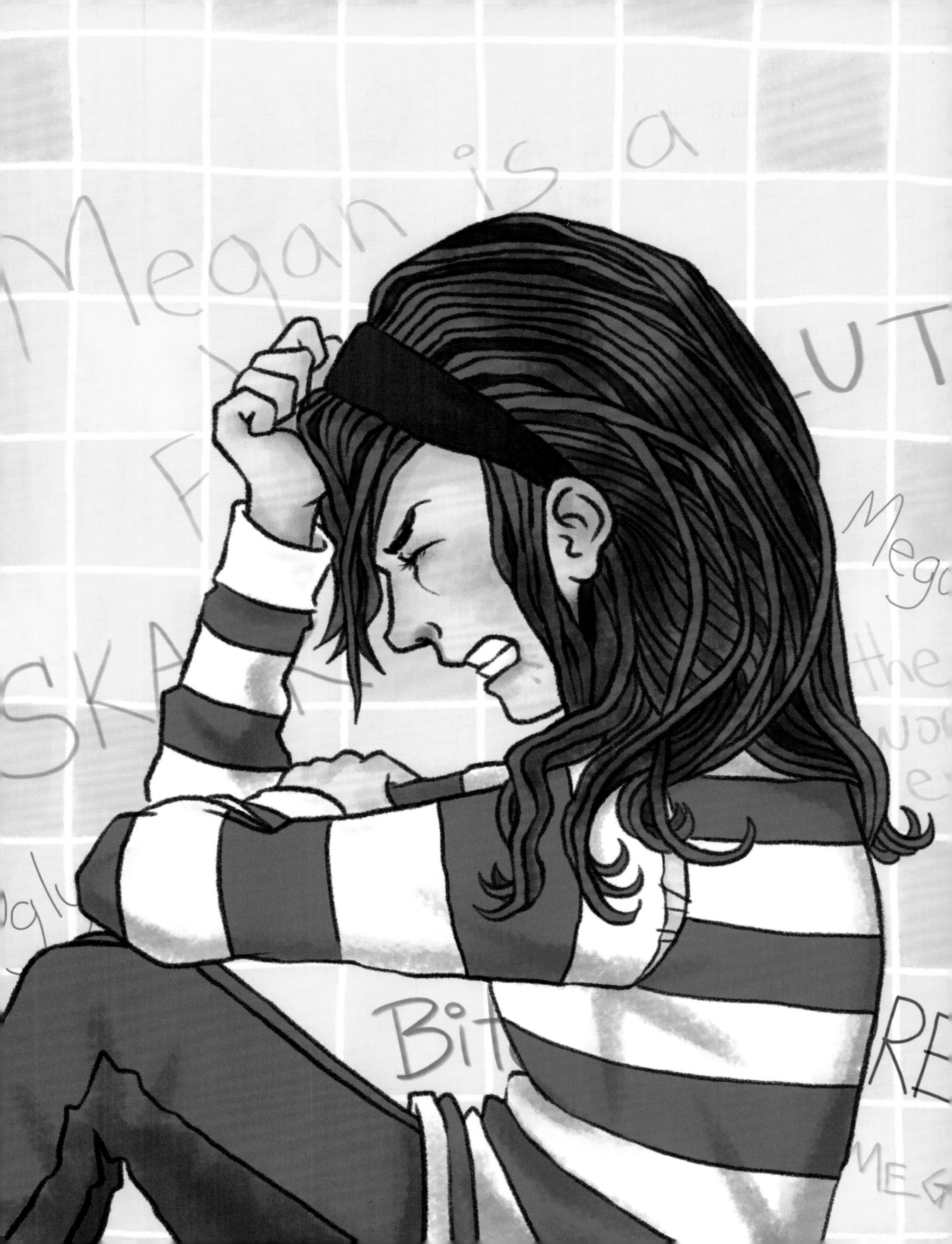

Megan is a
Megan

IT'S WHAT YOU

THROU

GETS YO

GO
GH that
where
YOU'RE
TO
GOING.

I MET THIS GUY. HE was the cutest guy ever, and I fell so in love with him. Every time I saw him, I just fell deeper in love with him. He was the biggest flirt ever—every girl fell for him. And this went on all throughout middle school. And all the way to my freshman year.

And it was tough. No matter how much we hung out or laughed together, he never felt the same way about me. I began feeling so bad about myself. Like if he didn't like

me, then what good was I? How come he didn't like me? What was wrong with me? Was I not pretty enough? Was I not nice enough? Maybe it was the way I talked? Finally, freshman year I couldn't take it anymore. I didn't feel happy when I was around him. I felt insecure. I just called him out on it. I told him about everything—my feelings and how I couldn't take it anymore. And he said he felt bad, but I was like a younger sister to him. Welp.

I was just chilling in my social studies class, kinda zoning out while trying to take notes, when suddenly we went off topic and my class was talking about illegal immigrants coming into the country, specifically Mexicans. My teacher started talking about how Mexicans bring illegal drugs into the country, and everyone started eyeing me. **YOU SEE, I WAS ONE OF THE ONLY HISPANICS IN MY SCHOOL, AND I WAS THE ONLY ONE IN THIS CLASS.** And then a boy in my class raised his hand and said, "But Mexicans are good hard workers, they aren't all bad." But then the teacher said, "Yes, but so are Americans, and you don't see them bringing in drugs." And I was just so shocked that a teacher would say this. **I WAS DUMBFOUNDED, SO ANGRY AND CONFUSED.** And the worst part is that I didn't do anything about it.

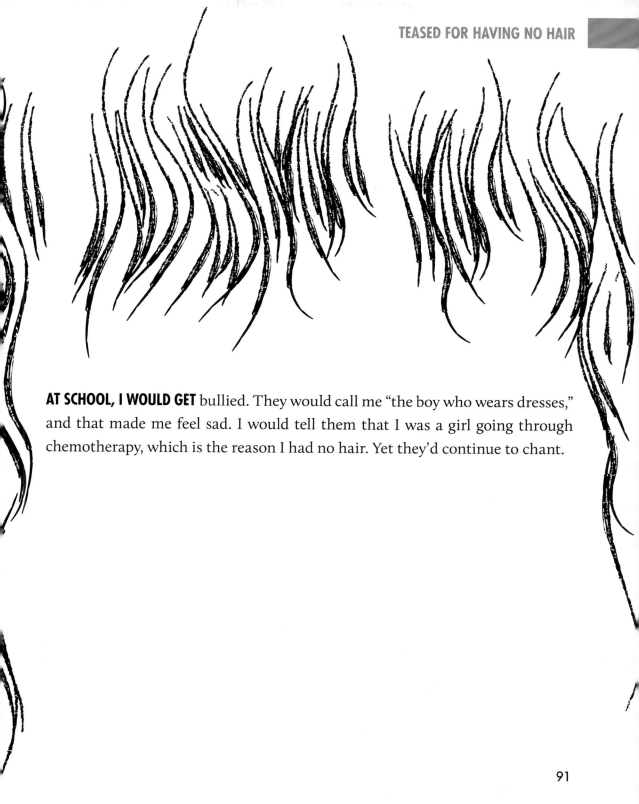

AT SCHOOL, I WOULD GET bullied. They would call me "the boy who wears dresses," and that made me feel sad. I would tell them that I was a girl going through chemotherapy, which is the reason I had no hair. Yet they'd continue to chant.

MY FRIEND AND I WERE JUST WALKING AROUND THE SCHOOL. WE'RE LIKE, WHAT SHOULD WE DO? BECAUSE WE HAD TEN MINUTES BEFORE THE BELL RANG. AND MY FRIEND SAID,

GIVE ME YOUR PHONE. I'M GONNA TURN ON AIRDROP.

SO WE'RE JUST SENDING PEOPLE MEMES, WALKING AROUND TO TRY AND FIND PEOPLE WHO HAVE AIRDROP ON.

AND WE HAVE FAKE NAMES. MINE'S "REBECCA'S PHONE." AND HERS IS "SALLY'S IPHONE."

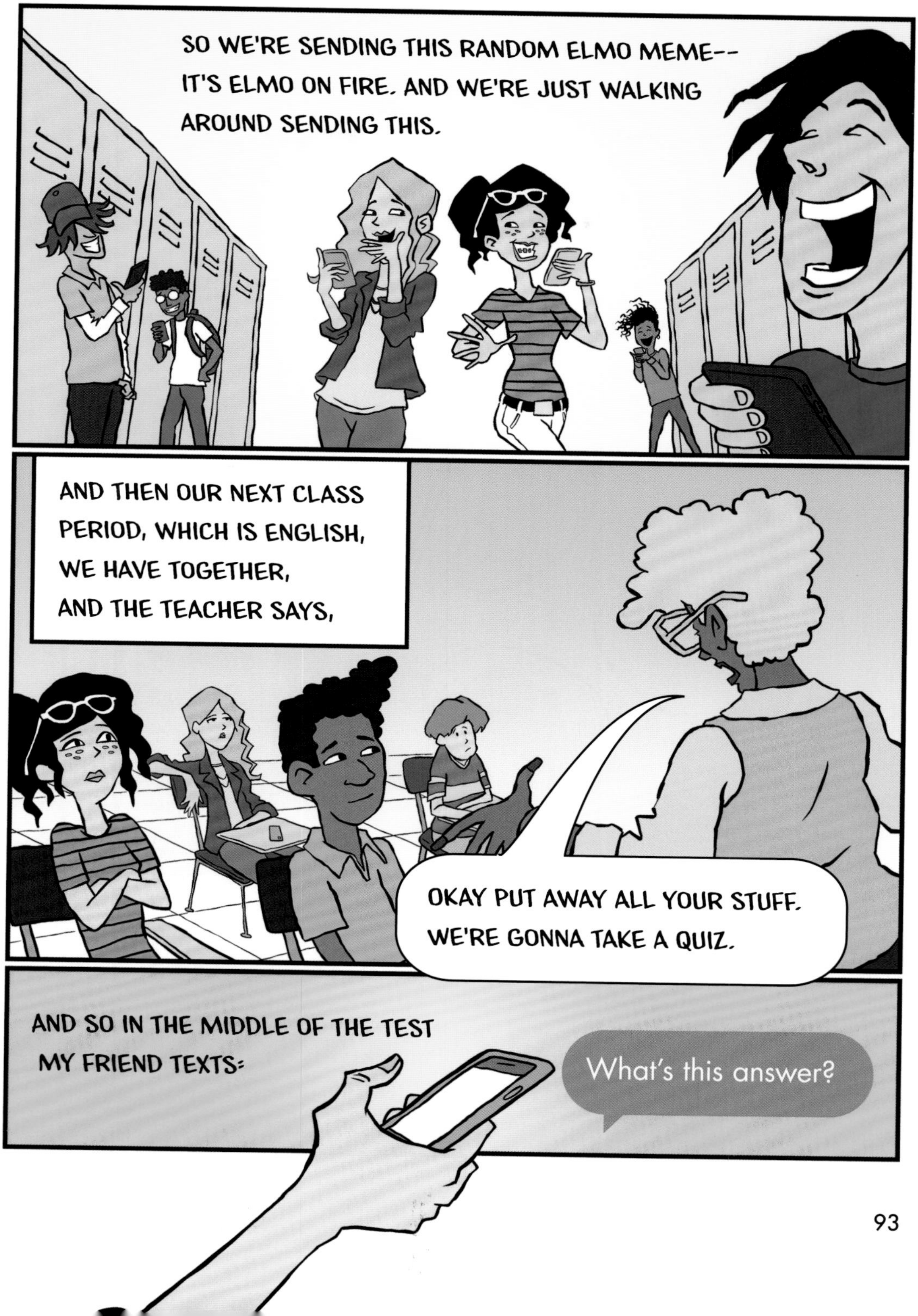
SO WE'RE SENDING THIS RANDOM ELMO MEME--
IT'S ELMO ON FIRE. AND WE'RE JUST WALKING
AROUND SENDING THIS.
AND THEN OUR NEXT CLASS
PERIOD, WHICH IS ENGLISH,
WE HAVE TOGETHER,
AND THE TEACHER SAYS,
OKAY PUT AWAY ALL YOUR STUFF.
WE'RE GONNA TAKE A QUIZ.
AND SO IN THE MIDDLE OF THE TEST
MY FRIEND TEXTS:
What's this answer?

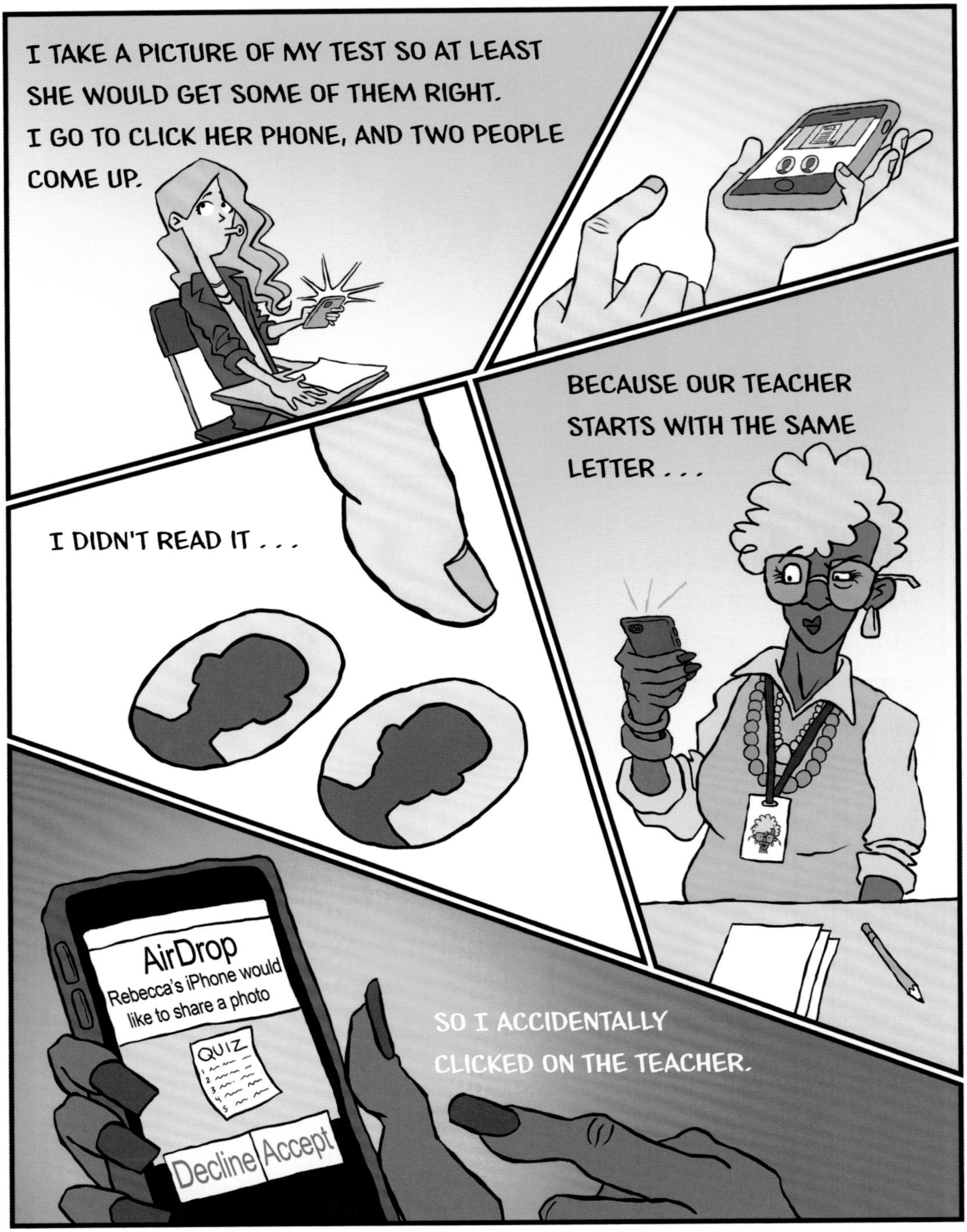
I TAKE A PICTURE OF MY TEST SO AT LEAST SHE WOULD GET SOME OF THEM RIGHT.
I GO TO CLICK HER PHONE, AND TWO PEOPLE COME UP.
BECAUSE OUR TEACHER STARTS WITH THE SAME LETTER . . .
I DIDN'T READ IT . . .
AirDrop
Rebecca's iPhone would like to share a photo
QUIZ
Decline
Accept
SO I ACCIDENTALLY CLICKED ON THE TEACHER.

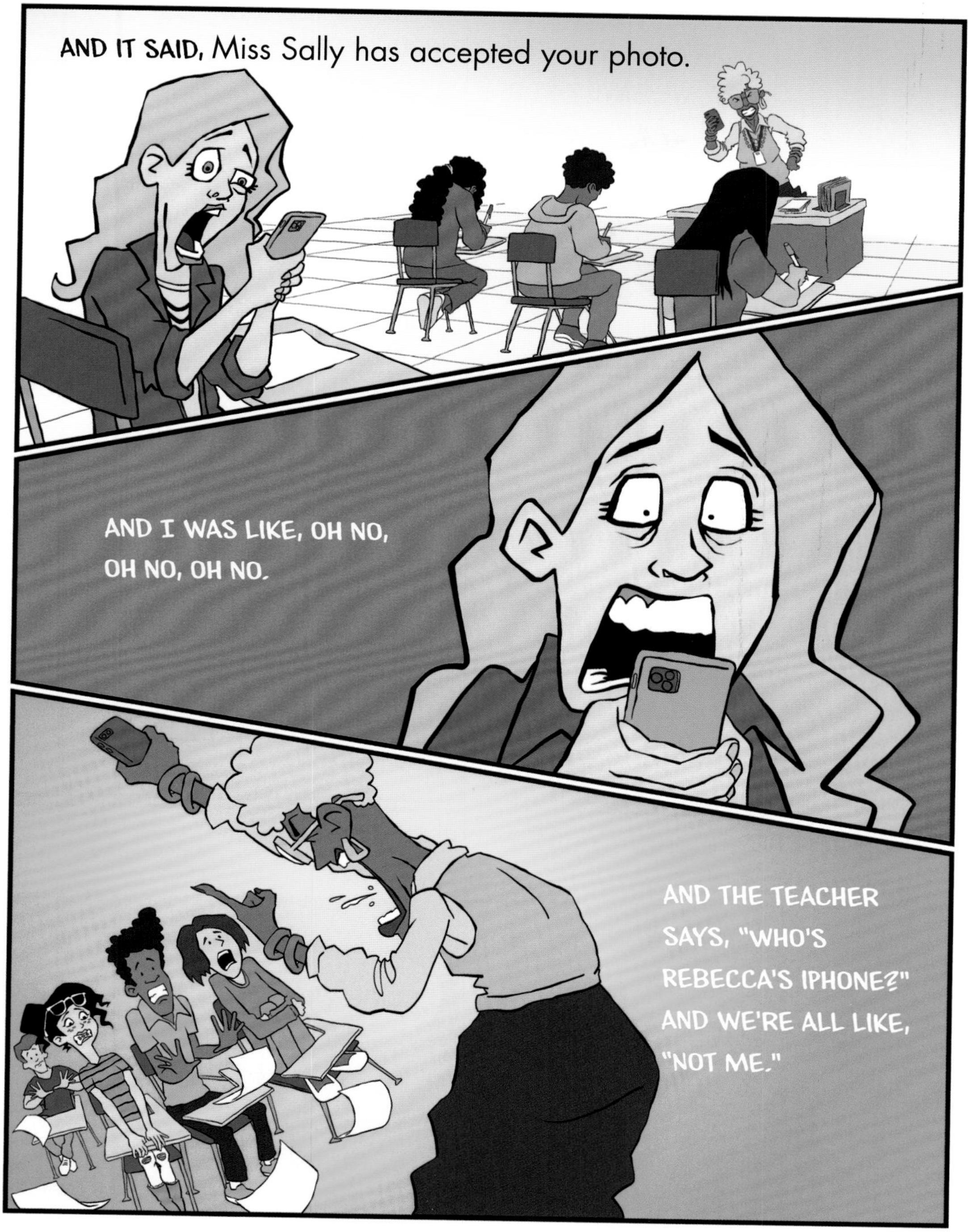
AND IT SAID, Miss Sally has accepted your photo.
AND I WAS LIKE, OH NO, OH NO, OH NO.
AND THE TEACHER SAYS, "WHO'S REBECCA'S IPHONE?" AND WE'RE ALL LIKE, "NOT ME."

AND SHE WAS GOING THROUGH OUR PHONES TO SEE IF WE HAVE AIRDROP ON.

SINCE MY FRIEND TURNED ON MY AIRDROP, I CAN'T FIND WHERE TO TURN OFF AIRDROP OR HOW TO CHANGE MY NAME.

SO THE TEACHER GOES THROUGH EVERYBODY'S SETTINGS AND LOOKS THROUGH. AND SHE GETS TO MINE. AND SHE SAYS,

COME WITH ME.

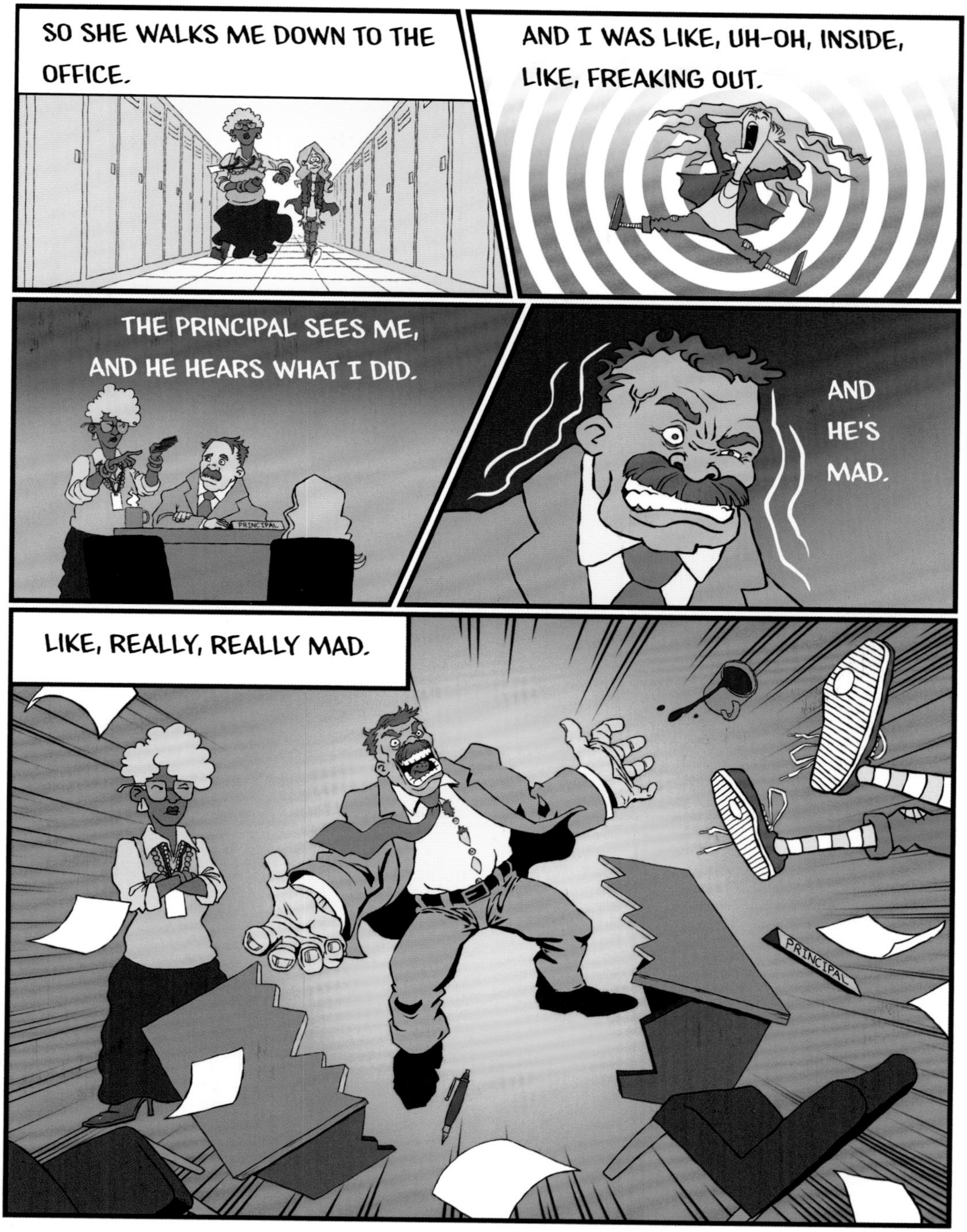
SO SHE WALKS ME DOWN TO THE OFFICE.
AND I WAS LIKE, UH-OH, INSIDE, LIKE, FREAKING OUT.
THE PRINCIPAL SEES ME, AND HE HEARS WHAT I DID.
AND HE'S MAD.
LIKE, REALLY, REALLY MAD.
PRINCIPAL

SO HE WAS LIKE, "WHY WOULD YOU DO THAT?"

"WHY DO YOU THINK THIS IS ACCEPTABLE?"

AND STUFF LIKE THAT.

THEN HE WAS LIKE, "WHO WAS THAT MEANT FOR?"

AND WITHOUT THINKING

I SAY MY FRIEND'S NAME.

AND I WAS LIKE, OH SHOOT.

SO HE CALLS MY FRIEND DOWN, AND HE CALLS OUR PARENTS.

WE ENDED UP GETTING SUSPENDED FOR THREE DAYS.

END OF STORY, WE FAILED THAT CLASS.

SO JUST DON'T AIRDROP PEOPLE ANSWERS TO A TEST. BECAUSE IF YOU DON'T LOOK QUICK ENOUGH, THEN YOU'RE GOING TO GET IN TROUBLE. OR JUST DON'T CHEAT AT ALL.

My anxiety is dragging me.
away from my friends.

When I was seven, my fat out. No good "I love you's,

MY TEACHER TOLD ME TO
TAKE OFF MY HIJAB.

I'm the worst at sports in my grade.

It turns out my best friend has been spreading rumors about me.

round six or

her walked

yes, no,

just gone....

The first year of my high school journey I was losing confidence in everything about myself and felt the urgent desire to change myself to fit in.

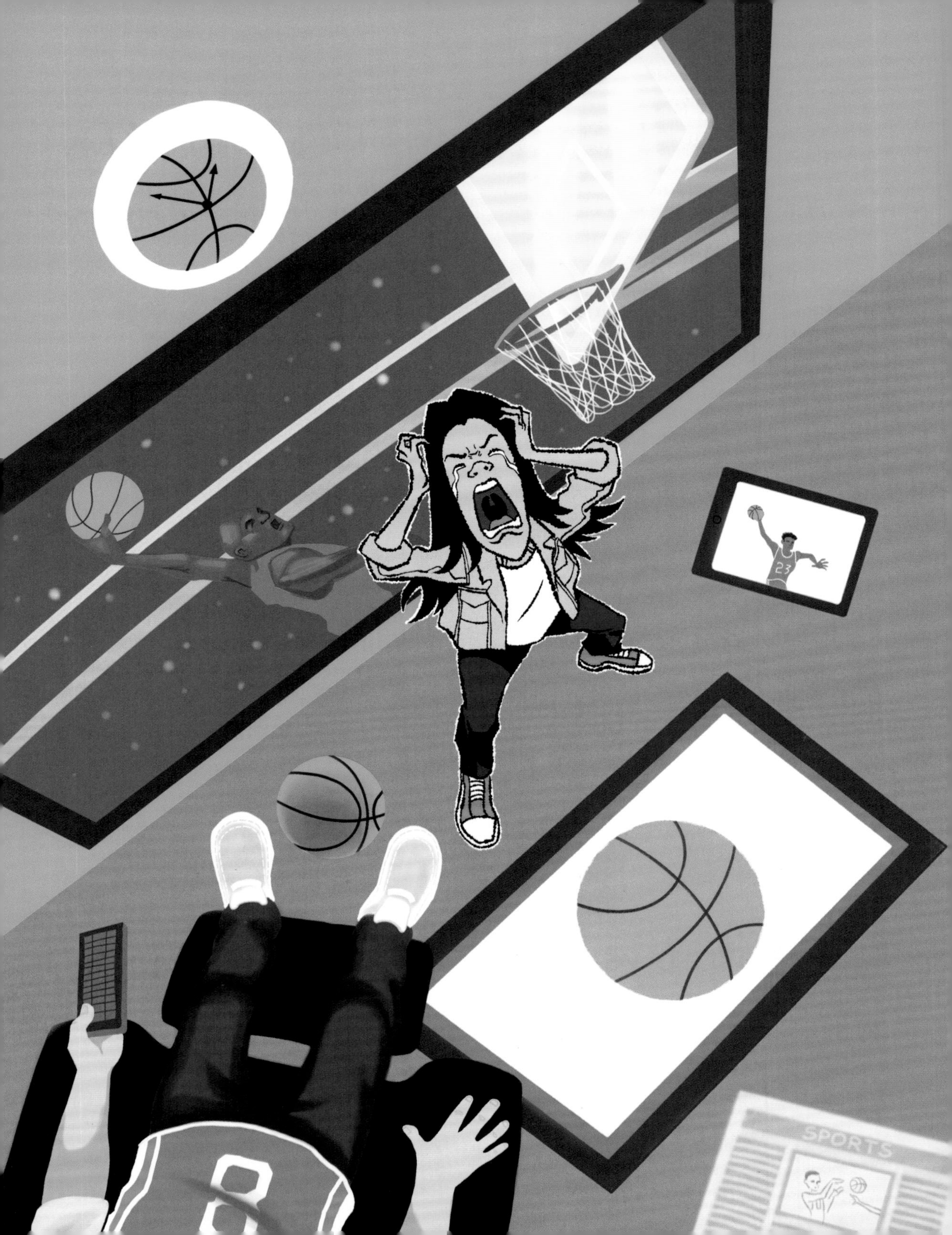
23
8
SPORTS

I NEVER HAVE TIME TO sing or act anymore. My time is so overwhelmed with basketball, basketball, basketball. My dad talks about it all the time, showing me basketball videos on YouTube, and it's so, so overwhelming. Sometimes I just need balance in my life, and I need them to know that singing is also a part of me and I don't want to leave it out. I want to have a say in my life. This is my life. Not theirs.

IT WAS A FRIDAY NIGHT, AND MY FRIEND AND I WERE LOOKING FOR SOMETHING TO DO. WE HAD ALREADY PLAYED BOARD GAMES, WATCHED MOVIES, HAD POPCORN, AND HAD SNACKS.

AT AROUND TWO IN THE MORNING, OUR FRIENDS TEXTED US AND ASKED IF WE WANTED TO GO TO A PARTY. WE WERE KIND OF HESITANT AT FIRST. WE SAID, "NO, WE'RE GOOD. WE'RE OKAY." THEN MY FRIEND CHANGED HER MIND AND SAID, "SURE, LET'S GO." ME? I WAS EXTREMELY HESITANT. I WAS SCARED.

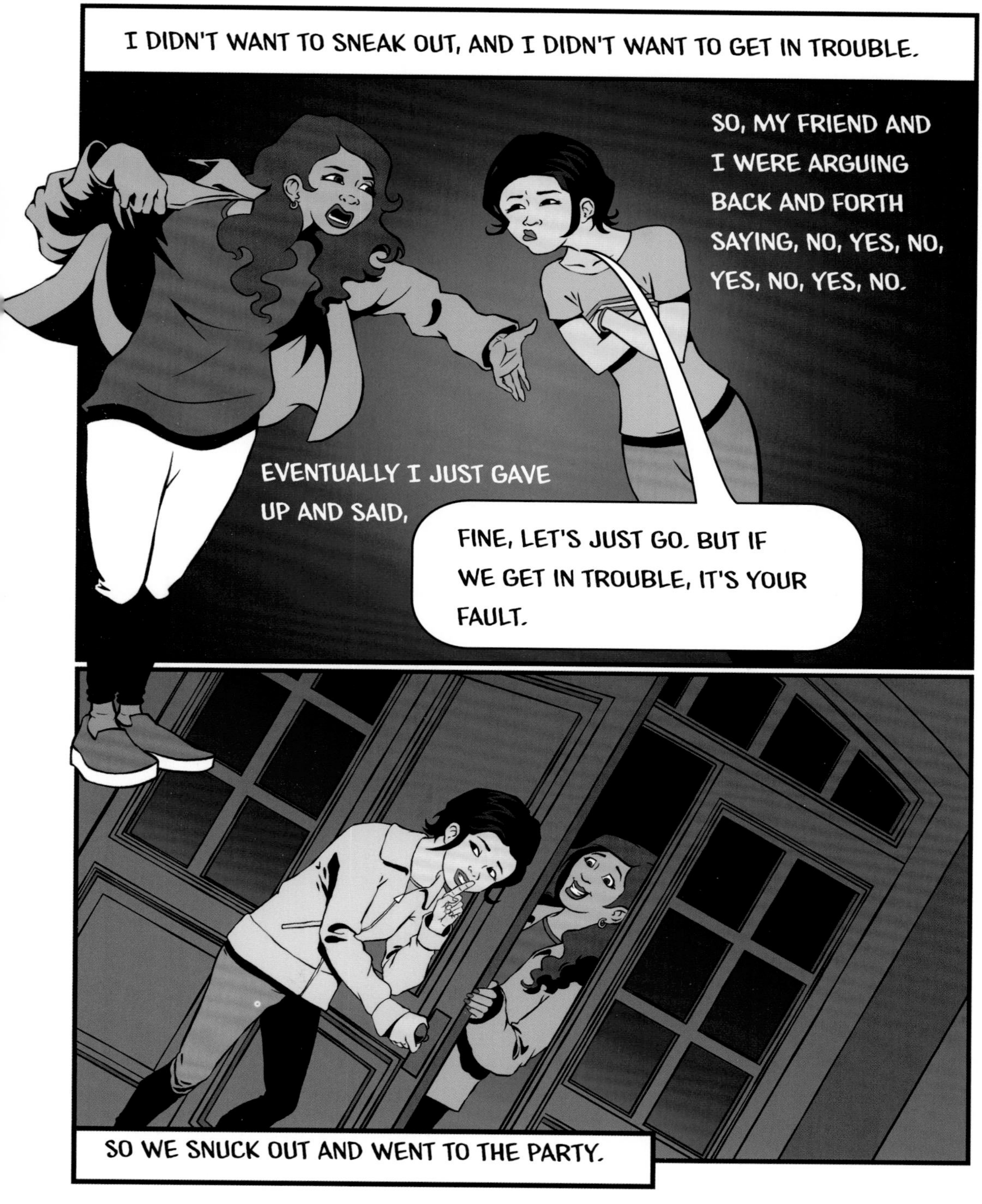
I DIDN'T WANT TO SNEAK OUT, AND I DIDN'T WANT TO GET IN TROUBLE.
SO, MY FRIEND AND I WERE ARGUING BACK AND FORTH SAYING, NO, YES, NO, YES, NO, YES, NO.
EVENTUALLY I JUST GAVE UP AND SAID,
FINE, LET'S JUST GO. BUT IF WE GET IN TROUBLE, IT'S YOUR FAULT.
SO WE SNUCK OUT AND WENT TO THE PARTY.

THERE WAS LOUD MUSIC PLAYING. THERE WERE A LOT OF PEOPLE THERE AND A LOT OF ALCOHOL AND DRUGS. THERE WERE A LOT OF GROWN PEOPLE THERE AS WELL.

SOMEONE OFFERED US A BEER. WE SAID NO. WE WERE SO HESITANT.

AND LIKE THIRTY SECONDS LATER, EVERYONE STARTED GATHERING AROUND US, CHANTING,

DRINK IT! DRINK IT! DRINK IT!

AND MY FRIEND AND I WOUND UP HAVING OUR FIRST BEER. AND OUR FIRST BEER TURNED INTO, LIKE, OUR ELEVENTH BEER.

THE POLICE WOUND UP GETTING CALLED BECAUSE THE NEXT-DOOR NEIGHBORS HAD A NOISE COMPLAINT.

MY FRIEND AND I WERE EXTREMELY INTOXICATED. THE OFFICER PUT US IN HANDCUFFS AND INTO THE BACK SEAT OF HIS CAR AND DROVE US DOWN TO THE POLICE STATION.

AND WE WERE IN THE POLICE STATION FOR ABOUT THIRTY MINUTES, UNTIL THEY FINALLY LET US CALL OUR MOMS. AND WE CALLED OUR MOMS, AND OUR MOMS WERE EXTREMELY FEROCIOUS. THEY WERE MAD. THEY YELLED AT US IN THE POLICE STATION, ON OUR WAY OUT OF THE POLICE STATION, AND ON THE CAR RIDE HOME. ON THE WAY TO BED, THEY WERE YELLING AT US. IN THE MORNING, THEY WERE YELLING AT US.

I LEARNED MY LESSON NOT TO SNEAK OUT AND NOT TO DO BAD THINGS AND DRINK UNDERAGE AND GET INTOXICATED. SO I GUESS THE MORAL OF THE STORY IS: DON'T EVER LET ANYONE PRESSURE YOU TO DO THINGS YOU'RE NOT READY FOR. DON'T.

We were at the dance, and I heard some kids laughing behind me. My friend's eyes widened and she stared down at me and whispered, "Look down." Nervously, I looked and saw that my legs and my dress were covered in blood. I had just gotten my period. **I LOOKED AROUND AND REALIZED EVERYONE WAS STARING AND LAUGHING AT ME.** I felt my face turn red. My friend quickly grabbed me and ran out of the gym. My other friends followed us to the bathroom, and we got a pad and called my mom. I was so embarrassed.

My mom picked me up, and on the way home I checked my Snapchat to see if anyone had posted anything. Some of the kids I'd added as friends and actually trusted took pictures of me in my bloody dress and tagged me on their stories. I was horrified.

I'M NOT VERY WEALTHY. WE have, like, phones and a roof over our heads, food and stuff, and clothes, but I don't have as much money as some of my other friends do. They all have the newest Jordans or always have new clothes and stuff. And I'll get a new pair of shoes or a new outfit like every once in a while, but I don't have all of the stuff that they do. And whenever somebody's like, "How come you don't have anything, like, new? How come you don't have any Jordans or anything?" I'm like, "Oh, I just don't like Jordans," because I'm so scared that people will continue to pick on me if I say that I don't have enough money to buy what I want.

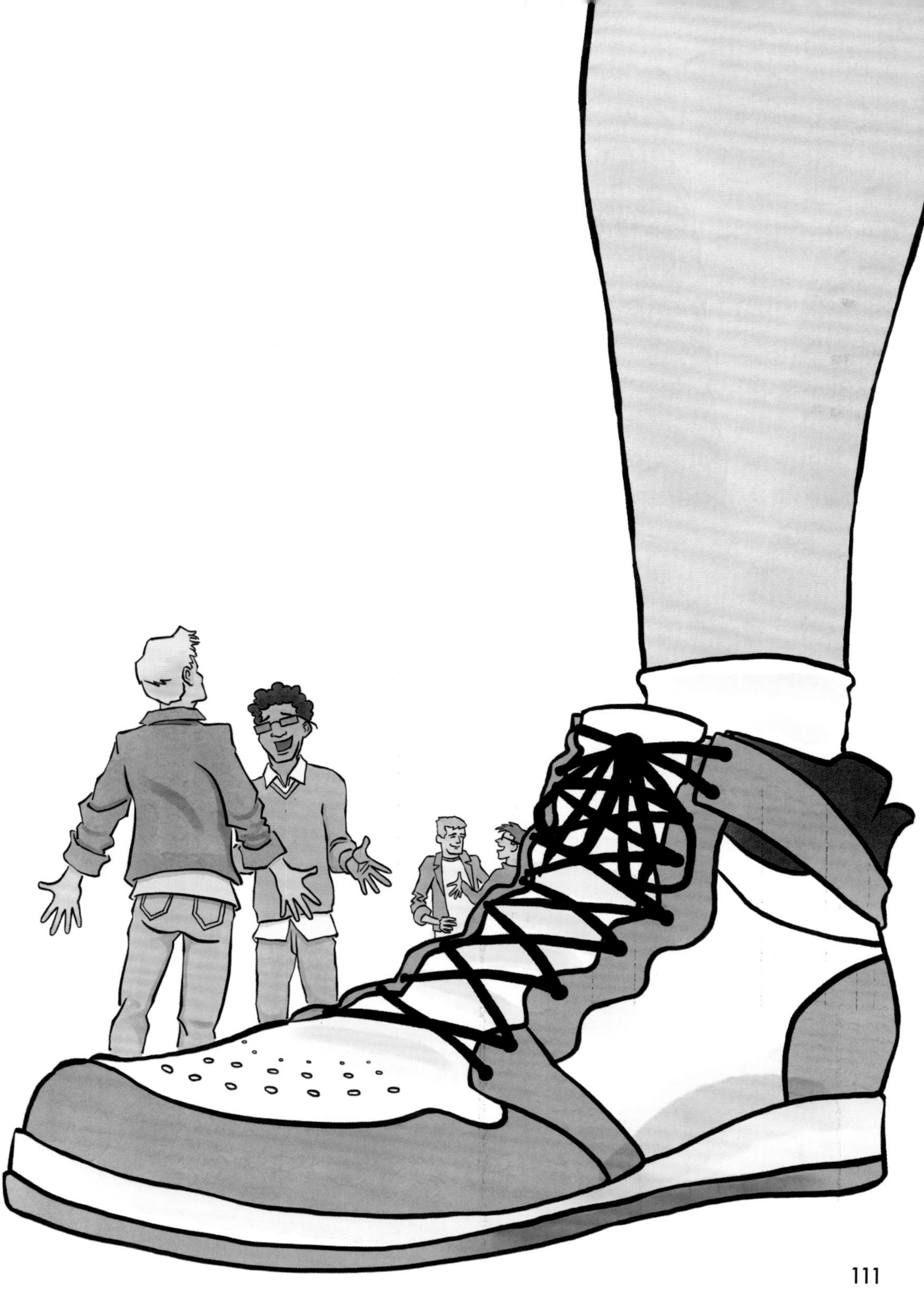

WHEN I WAS IN FIFTH GRADE, I LOST THE BEST FRIEND I EVER HAD TO CANCER. I NEVER GOT TO SAY GOODBYE, AND I PUSHED EVERYTHING DOWN SO I WOULDN'T FEEL IT ANYMORE. BUT IN THE SIXTH GRADE I DEVELOPED ANXIETY. I HAD MY FIRST PANIC ATTACK AND WAS TERRIFIED OUT OF MY MIND. A YEAR PASSED AND THINGS ONLY GOT WORSE. I GOT MORE AND MORE DEPRESSED. I WOKE UP SAD AND CRIED MYSELF TO SLEEP ALMOST EVERY NIGHT.

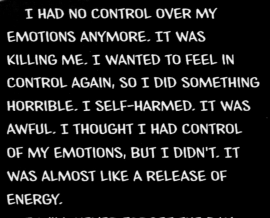

I HAD NO CONTROL OVER MY EMOTIONS ANYMORE. IT WAS KILLING ME. I WANTED TO FEEL IN CONTROL AGAIN, SO I DID SOMETHING HORRIBLE. I SELF-HARMED. IT WAS AWFUL. I THOUGHT I HAD CONTROL OF MY EMOTIONS, BUT I DIDN'T. IT WAS ALMOST LIKE A RELEASE OF ENERGY.

I WILL NEVER FORGET THE DAY MY MOM FOUND OUT. SHE PICKED ME UP FROM SCHOOL AND STARTED YELLING AT ME. SHE ASKED ME IF I WANTED TO GO TO A MENTAL HOSPITAL. THIS FREAKED ME OUT. I WAS ONLY THIRTEEN AT THE TIME. I TOLD HER NO AND LIED AND SAID I'D DONE IT FOR ATTENTION.

SHE LET IT GO, AND WE NEVER REALLY TALKED ABOUT IT AGAIN.

AFTER THAT I WAS MORE CAREFUL ABOUT IT. I CONTINUED TO DO IT, BUT NO ONE KNEW. I SPENT FRESHMAN YEAR OF HIGH SCHOOL IN THIS HORRIBLE LOOP OF HURTING MYSELF. BY SOPHOMORE YEAR, I REALIZED THAT IT HAD BECOME AN ADDICTION. I WAS DOING IT EVEN WHEN I WASN'T SAD. I JUST DID IT. MY ANXIETY HAD GOTTEN SO MUCH WORSE, AND THE WORST PART ABOUT IT ALL WAS THE LYING. I LIED TO MY FRIENDS AND FAMILY ABOUT EVERYTHING. IT WAS EXHAUSTING.

ONE NIGHT, I DECIDED ENOUGH WAS ENOUGH. I WAS SITTING IN MY BATHROOM ABOUT TO DO IT AGAIN, AND I HAD THIS IMAGE OF MY FRIEND WHO DIED OF CANCER AND HER FACE IF SHE FOUND OUT WHAT I WAS DOING. IT DEVASTATED ME. I IMMEDIATELY FLUSHED WHAT I USED TO HURT MYSELF AND WENT TO BED VOWING TO NEVER DO IT AGAIN.

THAT WAS THREE YEARS AGO.

I'M IN THERAPY FOR MY DEPRESSION AND ANXIETY, AND I'M DOING A LOT BETTER. I STILL NEED TO LEARN TO LIVE WITH THE SCARS I MADE, BUT THINGS HAVE BEEN GOING SO MUCH BETTER.

113

THE DAY BEFORE MY BOYFRIEND'S birthday I went and got a card and a gift. I was really looking forward to giving his presents to him at school. But that morning, I woke up and saw a bunch of messages from his brother asking if I had seen him, because his parents couldn't find him and they were about to call the police. I said, "No, he wasn't at my house, I haven't seen him," and you know I felt very worried. Right when I got to school, I was called to the office. I walked in and saw a room full of police officers. My parents were there, and they just looked at me and said, "Your boyfriend killed himself this morning." And I just started sobbing and saying, "This can't be true," but my parents said that the police found his body.

I went to his funeral, and I walked in and felt glued to the floor. I was so scared to see him in his coffin, but his brother took my hand. We walked in, and I saw him lying there looking peaceful and just like he always did, and I just cried.

I spent a lot of time thinking about how I could've done something or how I should have known that he was depressed and suicidal. I felt like it was somehow my fault. I got a lot of support from my friends, and they reassured me that I had done everything I could just by being there for him and dating him. I helped him, you know, maybe stay on earth for a little bit longer, and that thought really comforted me. When they had found him, he had been carrying a rock that I painted for him, and that just helped me and made me feel like I did do something good and that I did make his life better before he ended it.

WHEN *you* FEEL *like*

UP
ON E

GIVE LIF

GIVING
VERYTHING,
E A SECOND
chance.

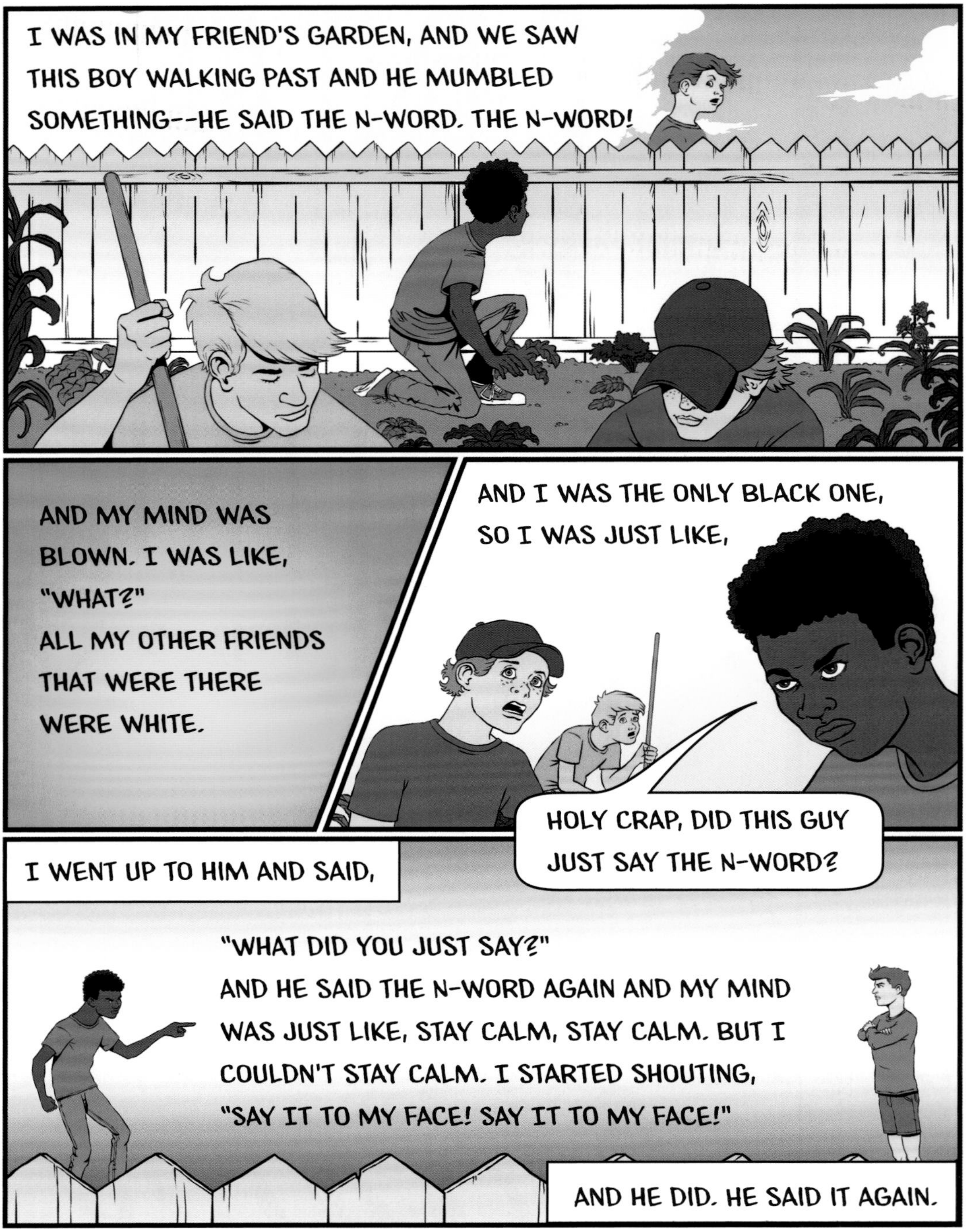
I WAS IN MY FRIEND'S GARDEN, AND WE SAW THIS BOY WALKING PAST AND HE MUMBLED SOMETHING--HE SAID THE N-WORD. THE N-WORD!
AND MY MIND WAS BLOWN. I WAS LIKE, "WHAT?" ALL MY OTHER FRIENDS THAT WERE THERE WERE WHITE.
AND I WAS THE ONLY BLACK ONE, SO I WAS JUST LIKE,
HOLY CRAP, DID THIS GUY JUST SAY THE N-WORD?
I WENT UP TO HIM AND SAID,
"WHAT DID YOU JUST SAY?" AND HE SAID THE N-WORD AGAIN AND MY MIND WAS JUST LIKE, STAY CALM, STAY CALM. BUT I COULDN'T STAY CALM. I STARTED SHOUTING, "SAY IT TO MY FACE! SAY IT TO MY FACE!"
AND HE DID. HE SAID IT AGAIN.

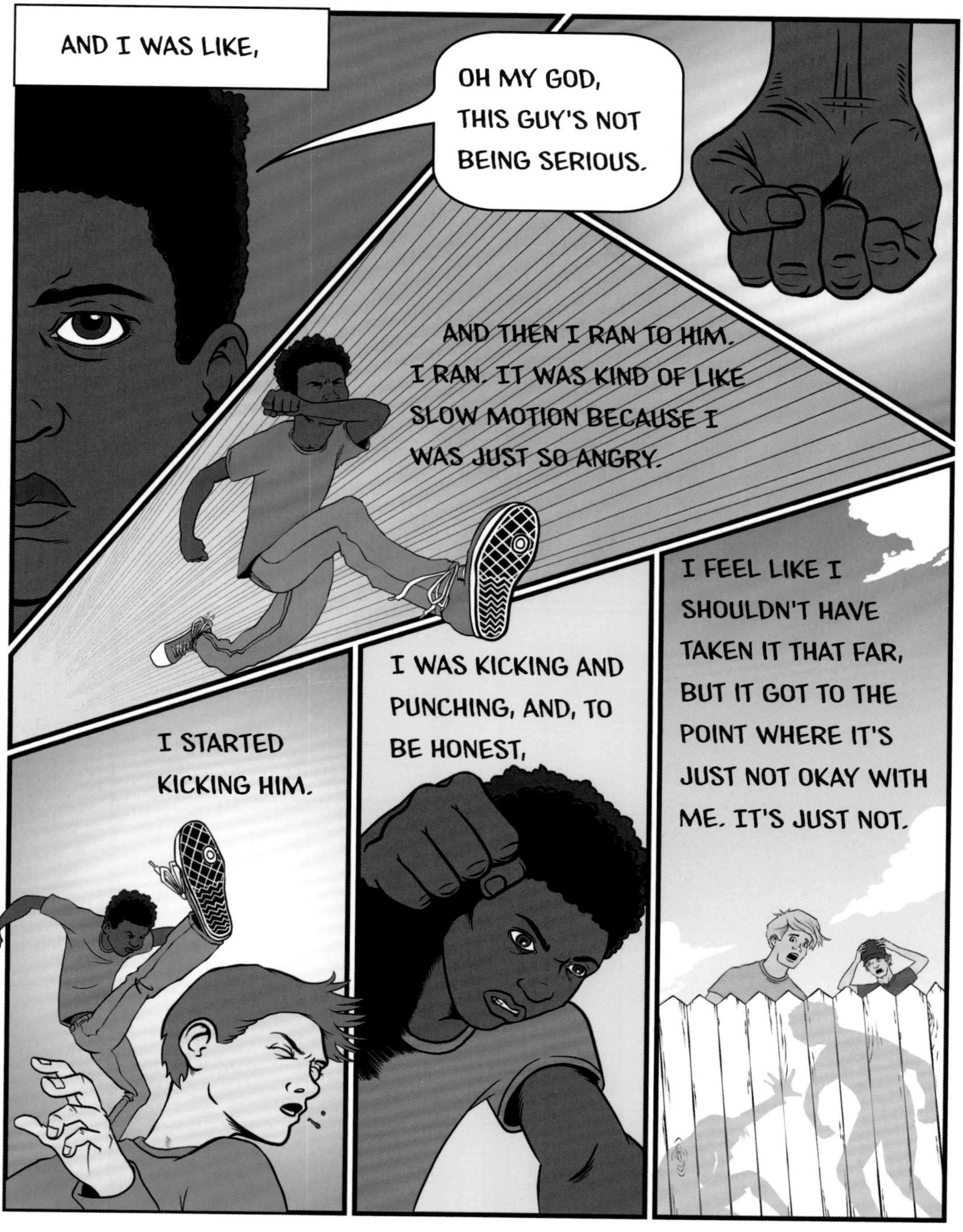
AND I WAS LIKE,
OH MY GOD, THIS GUY'S NOT BEING SERIOUS.
AND THEN I RAN TO HIM. I RAN. IT WAS KIND OF LIKE SLOW MOTION BECAUSE I WAS JUST SO ANGRY.
I STARTED KICKING HIM.
I WAS KICKING AND PUNCHING, AND, TO BE HONEST,
I FEEL LIKE I SHOULDN'T HAVE TAKEN IT THAT FAR, BUT IT GOT TO THE POINT WHERE IT'S JUST NOT OKAY WITH ME. IT'S JUST NOT.

HE WENT OFF CRYING AND TOLD HIS MOTHER, AND HIS MOM CAME OVER TO MY HOUSE AND TOLD MY MOM WHAT HAPPENED.

MY MOM WAS LIKE,

"OH MY GOD, YOU SHOULDN'T BE DOING THAT. EVEN THOUGH IT GETS THAT BAD, IT'S NOT THE WAY TO HANDLE SITUATIONS."

I FELT REALLY BAD AFTER, BUT STILL YOU DON'T CALL SOMEONE THAT WORD.

A FEW WEEKS AFTER, IT WAS STILL REALLY AWKWARD BETWEEN US. I DIDN'T APOLOGIZE FOR WHAT I DID.

BUT HE DID APOLOGIZE, AND I WAS JUST LIKE,

YOU DON'T SAY STUFF LIKE THAT TO A BLACK PERSON. IT'S NOT OKAY.

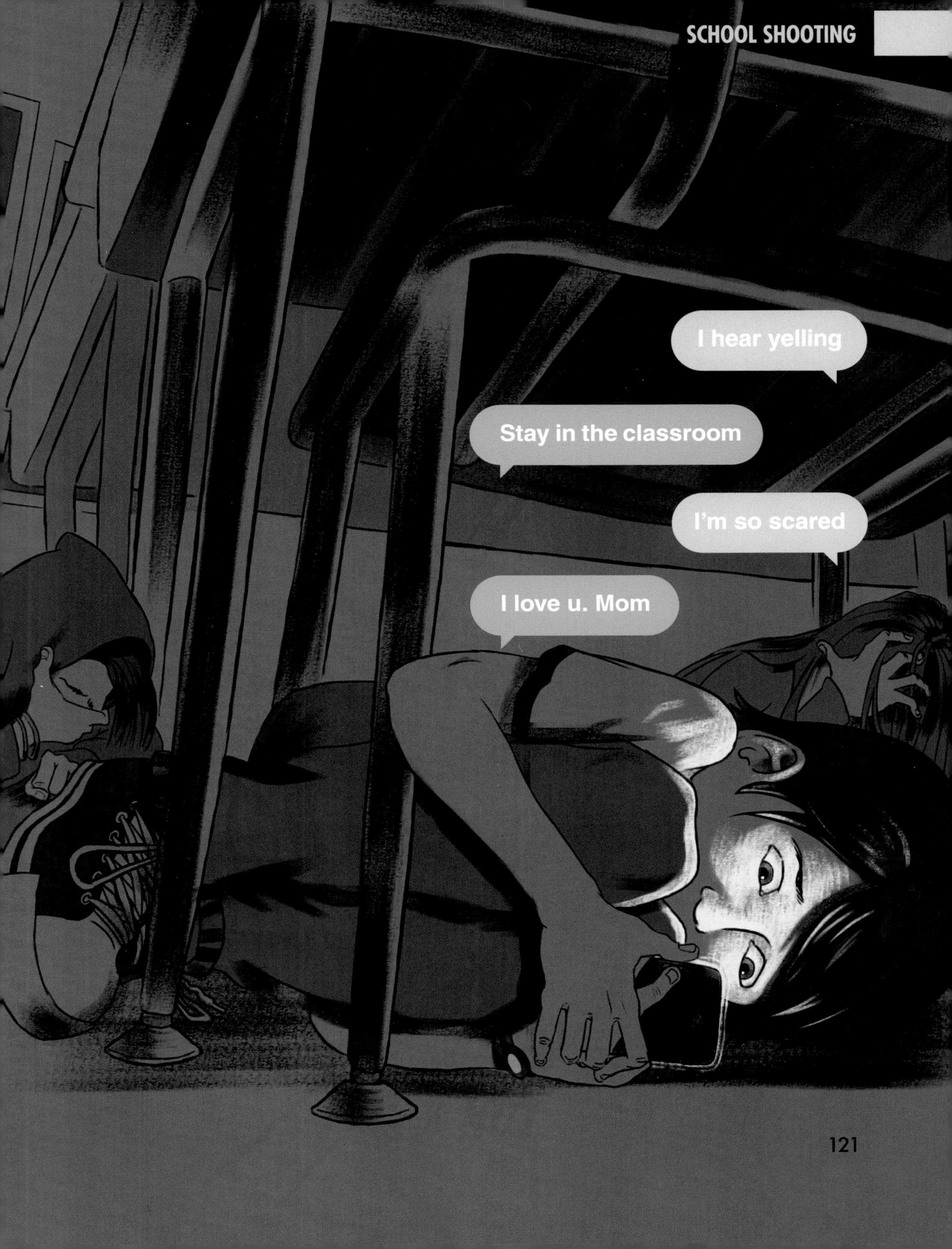
I hear yelling
Stay in the classroom
I'm so scared
I love u. Mom

IT ALL STARTED WHEN I WAS EIGHT. As I was growing up, I realized my mom wasn't like other moms. She was older, and her hair was a little gray. Once I asked her how old she was, but she didn't respond. So I asked my friends how old their moms were, and they all said thirty, thirty-five, you know, in their thirties.

So I tried asking my mom her age so many times until she gave up one day and just said she was fifty-eight. And, well, I was in complete shock 'cause I never imagined her to be that old given my age. And there's nothing wrong with her being fifty-eight or anything. But I asked her, **"I CAME FROM YOU, RIGHT? YOU HAD ME?"** And she said she didn't. She confessed that I actually was adopted and said she wanted to tell me when I was a little older.

From that day on, I was completely scared that if I misbehaved and got on my mom's last nerve, she would put me up for adoption again. I didn't know what to do if I ever got mad at her or she got mad at me. Do I just like stand there or what do I do? One day, we actually did get into a fight, and I'm like, "Please don't put me up for adoption. I don't wanna go back. I'm scared." And she said she would never do that to me 'cause she loved me and she was my forever mom. I felt safe again, and even though I was mad that my mom didn't tell me sooner, I love her and am so lucky she is my mom.

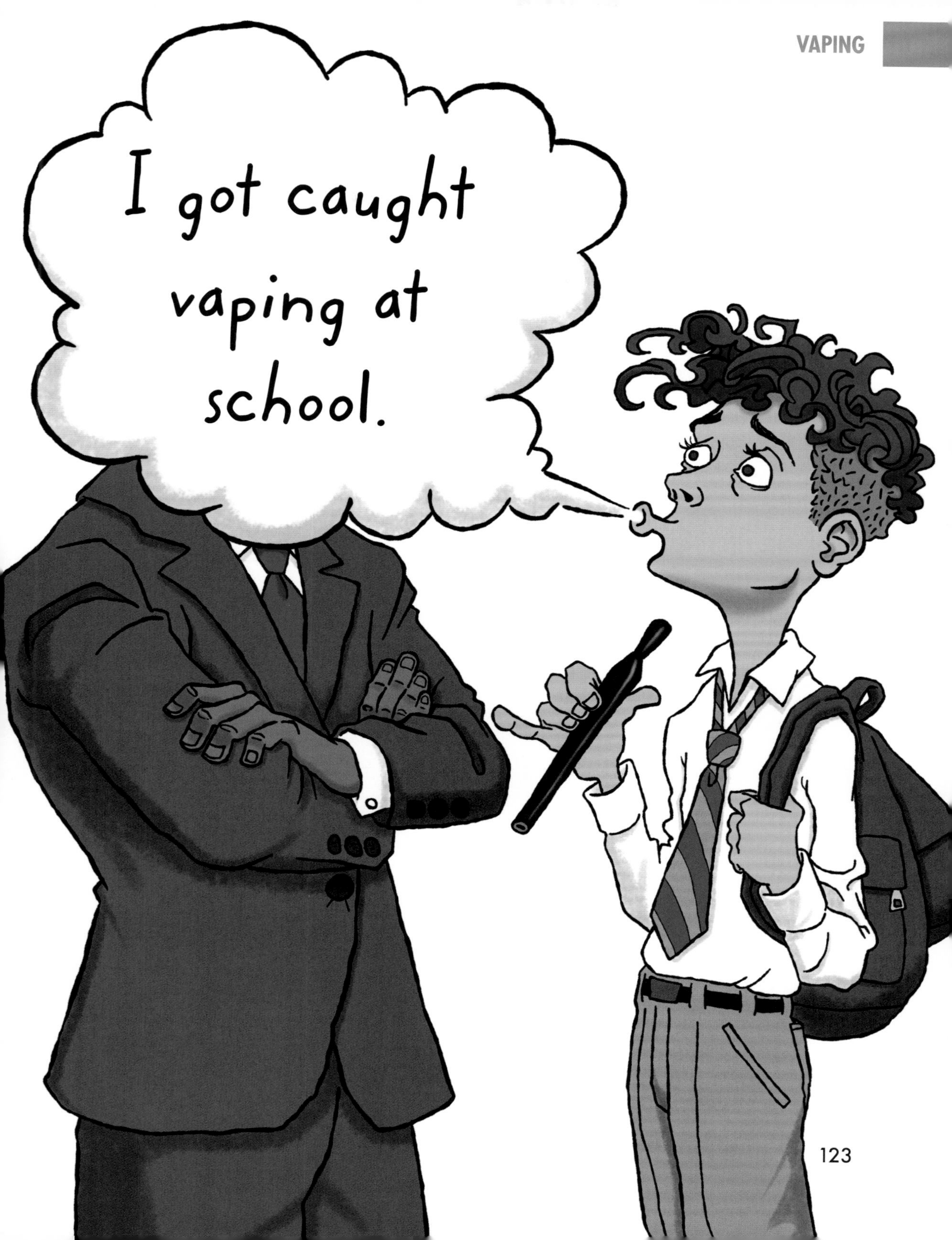
I got caught vaping at school.

WHEN I WAS SIXTEEN YEARS OLD, I HAD MY FIRST BOYFRIEND. I THOUGHT HE WAS A PRETTY GREAT GUY, EVEN THOUGH SOMETIMES I FELT LIKE OUR RELATIONSHIP WAS MOVING A LITTLE TOO FAST FOR ME.

HE ALWAYS PRESSURED ME TO DO THINGS I DIDN'T WANT TO DO. ONE TIME WE WERE JUST SITTING AROUND WATCHING TV ON MY BED WHILE MY PARENTS WERE AT WORK.

HE TOOK THE REMOTE AND TURNED THE TV OFF AND STARTED TELLING ME WHAT HE WANTED US TO DO TOGETHER.

AND I JUST TOLD HIM, "PLEASE STOP, I'M NOT READY TO DO THIS." HE GOT KIND OF MAD AND SAID HE WOULD LEAVE ME IF I DIDN'T DO WHAT HE WANTED ME TO DO.

SO I WAS FACED WITH A CHOICE THAT I'D REGRET FOR THE REST OF MY LIFE. I ENDED UP DOING WHAT HE WANTED.

FAST-FORWARD ABOUT A MONTH AND I STARTED FEELING DIFFERENT. I WAS CRAVING DIFFERENT FOODS THAT I USUALLY WOULDN'T EAT.

I ALWAYS NEEDED TO PEE AND SOMETIMES FELT NAUSEATED. I STARTED THROWING UP EVERY DAY.

FINALLY, I TOLD MY BEST FRIEND. SHE LOOKED AT ME AND ASKED,

HAVE YOU DONE ANYTHING LATELY?

I SAID,

WHAT DO YOU MEAN?

AND THEN I REMEMBERED THAT NIGHT. I WAS LIKE, "YES. YES I DID."

WE WENT TO THE PHARMACY AND GOT A PREGNANCY TEST. I TOOK THE TEST, AND IT WAS POSITIVE.

MY FRIEND JUST HUGGED ME AS I CRIED.

I WENT THROUGH A LOT AFTER THAT DAY.

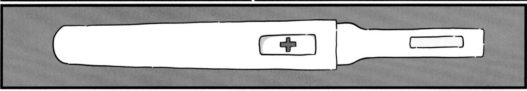

I WAS KICKED OUT OF MY HOUSE BECAUSE I WAS PREGNANT.

AND I LEARNED QUITE A LESSON--YOU SHOULD NEVER BE PRESSURED INTO DOING ANYTHING YOU DON'T WANT TO DO.

TODAY I HAVE MY DAUGHTER.
SHE IS THREE YEARS OLD, AND I DON'T REGRET HAVING HER, BUT I DO REGRET HAVING HER AT THE TIME I DID. IT WAS MUCH MORE DIFFICULT FOR ME.

As a teenager who is fighting with depression,
I hide it by smiling and making others laugh
so that nobody can see the struggles of my battle
with anxiety and bad thoughts.

I struggled to n

people so I wo

library to eat n

library was full

lunch in a bath

I threw up in the middle of the
hallway at school.

I LET MY FRIEND WALK ALL OVER ME.

Whenever my grandma comes to visit she criticizes my weight and calls me fat.

eet new

ld sit in the

y lunch. If the

I'd eat my

oom stall.

I failed my driving test . . . again.

We're homeless, and every day we're fighting to find a place to sleep, find somewhere where we can feel safe and not have to worry about bad people trying to harm us. For the past five years we've been hopping from place to place, trying to stay with friends of my parents or staying at shelters that my mom applied to. Once we had to sleep in an abandoned shed and once in our car. And it sucks. It really does.

Every day it's an emotional toll to be able to keep it together and be happy, be positive for my mother and father, for my siblings, and just try to help us get through this. My mother, she's kind of a mess. She's doing her best to stay strong for us, but I can see it. She's beginning to break down and not do so well. She is managing to keep us safe and warm and fed, but mentally she's just panicking. And my father, he's always working from morning to night, but his checks aren't that great. Actually, they are great, we just don't really have much to spend after paying for gas and such.

WE'VE BEEN TRYING TO STAY STRONG, TRYING TO BE OKAY AND WORK TOGETHER.

To those out there who are dealing with the same situation, just know it will get better eventually. Stay positive, stay happy, and keep each other in line, you know. I'm still homeless, but I'm happy. My family's still okay, and we love each other. And to me, I feel as if that's all that really matters.

I FOUND OUT THAT SOMEONE recorded a video of me and my friend at the party and posted it on Instagram. It was really embarrassing 'cause it was on this Instagram page where they post college kids going crazy. It was up for like two or three days, just getting more and more views, more and more comments, and people were starting to recognize me from it. It was so embarrassing, and I just wanted to turn invisible.

MY DAD AND I HAD to get backyard supplies to do our yard, and there was a line. As we got in line I kept hearing this couple whisper that Chinese people were the cause of COVID-19 and saying that we need to go back to our country.

I was in the parking lot in my dad's car waiting for him to get out of the store. I rolled the window down to get some air and right next to us was this elderly woman. As soon as I rolled the window down, she glared at me and rolled all of her windows up and tried covering her mouth in gasps as if I were a monster.

I NOTICED THAT MY GROUP of friends were much thinner than I was, and I started feeling really self-conscious about my body. I decided I needed to lose weight. I started exercising a lot and dieting. Weeks passed, and I rapidly shed the weight. I started noticing huge changes. At first, I loved the results. I was slim-thick. But I felt like it wasn't enough. I wanted to keep getting skinnier. I always saw this fat person in the mirror, so when I finally saw myself skinny, I didn't want to stop.

So I kept going with my unhealthy habit of dieting and excessively exercising. Working out an hour a day turned to three hours. I became more and more obsessive with food and my weight each day. I decided to skip breakfast and then it became skipping breakfast and lunch.

Then I decided to skip breakfast, lunch, and even dinner sometimes.

DON'T EAT!
DON'T EAT!
DON'T EAT!
DON'T EAT!
DON'T EAT!
DON'T EAT!
DON'T EAT!
DON'T EAT!
DON'T EAT!
DON'T EAT!
DON'T EAT!
DON'T EAT!

My parents got worried because they started to notice my weight loss. They took me to my doctor, and he said, "If you keep going, you're going to be diagnosed with anorexia." That scared me because I had friends who had died from anorexia and bulimia, and I didn't want to be like that. I needed to gain weight because it was unhealthy to be this skinny.

And it's hard. It's really hard because once you stop eating for that amount of time, your body rejects food. So every time I eat like one meal I'm done for the day. But I'm trying really hard to gain weight.

So please, if you think you want to lose weight, don't ever starve yourself. I don't want to die, and I don't want anyone else to suffer because it's really hard to get back to where you were.

I'm trying to get better. I'm slowly getting better.

WHEN I WAS A SOPHOMORE, MY BOYFRIEND BROUGHT A WEED BROWNIE TO SCHOOL.

BEFORE CLASSES STARTED, I SAID,

OKAY. LET'S TAKE IT.

I WAS FOOLISH BECAUSE I'D NEVER TAKEN A WEED BROWNIE BEFORE, SO I DIDN'T KNOW HOW THEY WORKED OR HOW THEY AFFECT YOU.

I TOOK A LITTLE LESS THAN HALF AND I FELT FINE. BUT IN FIRST PERIOD I STARTED FEELING A LITTLE WOOZY, AND I STARTED LAUGHING AT EVERYTHING. I WENT TO THE GIRLS' LOCKER ROOM, AND THE WHOLE ROOM STARTED GOING IN CIRCLES.

I STARTED GETTING DIZZY, AND I FELT AS IF I WERE ON A BOAT. I COULDN'T STAND UP STRAIGHT. I WAS FREAKING OUT.

MY MOUTH WAS GETTING SO DRY, AS IF THERE WERE SANDPAPER IN IT. THE WHOLE ROOM STARTED GOING AROUND AND AROUND AND IN SLOW MOTION.

MY TEACHER WALKED UP TO ME IN SLOW MOTION, AND HE SAID,

ARE YOU OKAY?

AND I SAID,

NO. CAN I PLEASE GO TO THE NURSE?

139

ONCE I GOT TO THE NURSE, SHE SAT ME DOWN AND GOT ME ICE-COLD WATER. SHE ASKED ME,

WHAT DO YOU FEEL? HAVE YOU TAKEN ANY MEDICATION?

AND ME, NOT BEING IN THE RIGHT STATE OF MIND, SAID,

I ATE A WEED BROWNIE THIS MORNING.

SO SHE FREAKED OUT AND CALLED THE VICE PRINCIPAL IN, AND THE VICE PRINCIPAL WAS MAD. BUT ALL I REMEMBER WAS HOLDING HER HAND BECAUSE I THOUGHT I WAS GOING TO FALL OFF THE TWO-FOOT-TALL CHAIR I WAS SITTING ON.

WHEN MY MOM GOT THERE TO PICK ME UP, SHE WAS SO MAD.

ON THE WAY HOME, I WAS CRYING AND SOBBING, AND STILL EVERYTHING WAS GOING IN SLOW MOTION.

DO I REGRET IT? YES.

I've made
and I've r
things, bu
thing is th
helped me

mistakes

gretted

the best

t it has

grow??

SO MY FRIEND AND I were sitting in the gym, and we decided to play a little joke on guys we didn't know by making a fake Instagram account. We set the profile picture as a girl we didn't know. She was a model. I knew nobody really knew her because she wasn't that famous. And a lot of guys started rolling in like, "Wow, you're gorgeous. Hey, can I get your number? What's your name, beautiful?" Things that guys never said to me. I enjoyed it, so we continued doing it, just playing jokes throughout the whole school day.

When I got home I was thinking, I'm going to make a new account, because I enjoyed the attention I got with my friend. I made the account and started talking to guys I didn't know, lying about my age, telling them I was seventeen when I was really thirteen. I got a lot of graphic messages. They were all very sexual.

Then I got caught. My mom went through

my phone, and she was asking me, "Why would you do this? This is creepy. You shouldn't be using pictures of a girl you don't know." I didn't want to tell her that the real reason why I did this was that I felt like it was the only way I could get any attention from boys.

IN NINTH GRADE I HAD A BIG CRUSH ON THIS SOPHOMORE. HE WAS SMART, TALL, AND HANDSOME, AND THE GIRLS IN MY GRADE WERE ALL OVER HIM.

VALENTINE'S DAY WAS COMING UP, AND I DECIDED TO CONFESS MY FEELINGS TO HIM. I WROTE HIM A NOTE AND SLID IT IN HIS GYM LOCKER.

EVERYTHING WAS GOING SMOOTHLY UNTIL LUNCH, WHEN I SAW HIM READING THE LETTER OUT LOUD.

HE STARTED LAUGHING AND YELLING,

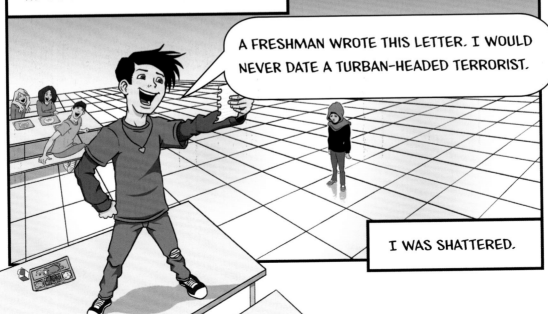

A FRESHMAN WROTE THIS LETTER. I WOULD NEVER DATE A TURBAN-HEADED TERRORIST.

I WAS SHATTERED.

My mom's a good mom by day, but it goes downhill at night when the drinking starts. Usually the next day she doesn't remember what happened the night before, which makes me more upset. She's an adult, so who am I to tell her what to do? But she will always be my mom and I love her a lot, even though her drinking obsession is hurting me.

I REMEMBER MY FIRST DAY OF HIGH SCHOOL. IT WAS REALLY SCARY. IT WAS A NEW SCHOOL WITH NEW PEOPLE, AND I WAS REALLY SHY. I TRIED TO OVERCOME MY SHYNESS SO I COULD BECOME POPULAR.

MY GOAL WAS TO BECOME ONE OF THE COOL KIDS, JOIN A SPORTS TEAM, AND GET INVITED TO PARTIES, YOU KNOW?

ONE DAY AT LUNCH I TRIED TO FIND SOMEWHERE TO SIT, AND I SAT WITH THE COOL KIDS.

THEY ALL GLARED AT ME, AND THEY THOUGHT IT WAS STRANGE FOR ME TO SIT AT THEIR TABLE 'CAUSE AT MY SCHOOL, I WAS SORT OF KNOWN AS THE WEIRDO. I TRIED TO JOIN THEIR CONVERSATION, BUT THEY ALL IGNORED ME.

THE NEXT DAY, ONE OF THE COOL KIDS--SHE WAS LIKE ONE OF THE MOST POPULAR GIRLS IN SCHOOL-- ASKED ME IF I WANTED TO HANG OUT WITH HER AFTER SCHOOL.

I WAS CONFUSED ABOUT WHY SHE WAS TALKING TO ME, BUT I SAID YEAH.

WE BECAME REALLY CLOSE AFTERWARD. WE SHARED SECRETS.

WE HUNG OUT AFTER SCHOOL, WENT TO THE MALL AND MOVIES AND PARTIES, AND IT FELT REALLY GREAT. IT JUST FELT NICE TO HAVE ALL THE ATTENTION.

BUT I SORT OF CHANGED. I STARTED TO BECOME LIKE A REALLY MEAN, AWFUL PERSON. I WAS REALLY MEAN TO PEOPLE, AND I THOUGHT THAT MAYBE IT WAS MY FRIEND WHO CHANGED ME BECAUSE SHE WAS REALLY MEAN TO PEOPLE.

I ASKED HER ONE DAY WHY SHE WANTED TO BE MY FRIEND.

SHE SAID SHE FELT SORRY FOR ME AND WANTED TO HELP ME TRY TO BECOME COOL INSTEAD OF THIS WEIRD LOSER LONER.

I DIDN'T KNOW HOW TO REACT TO THAT.

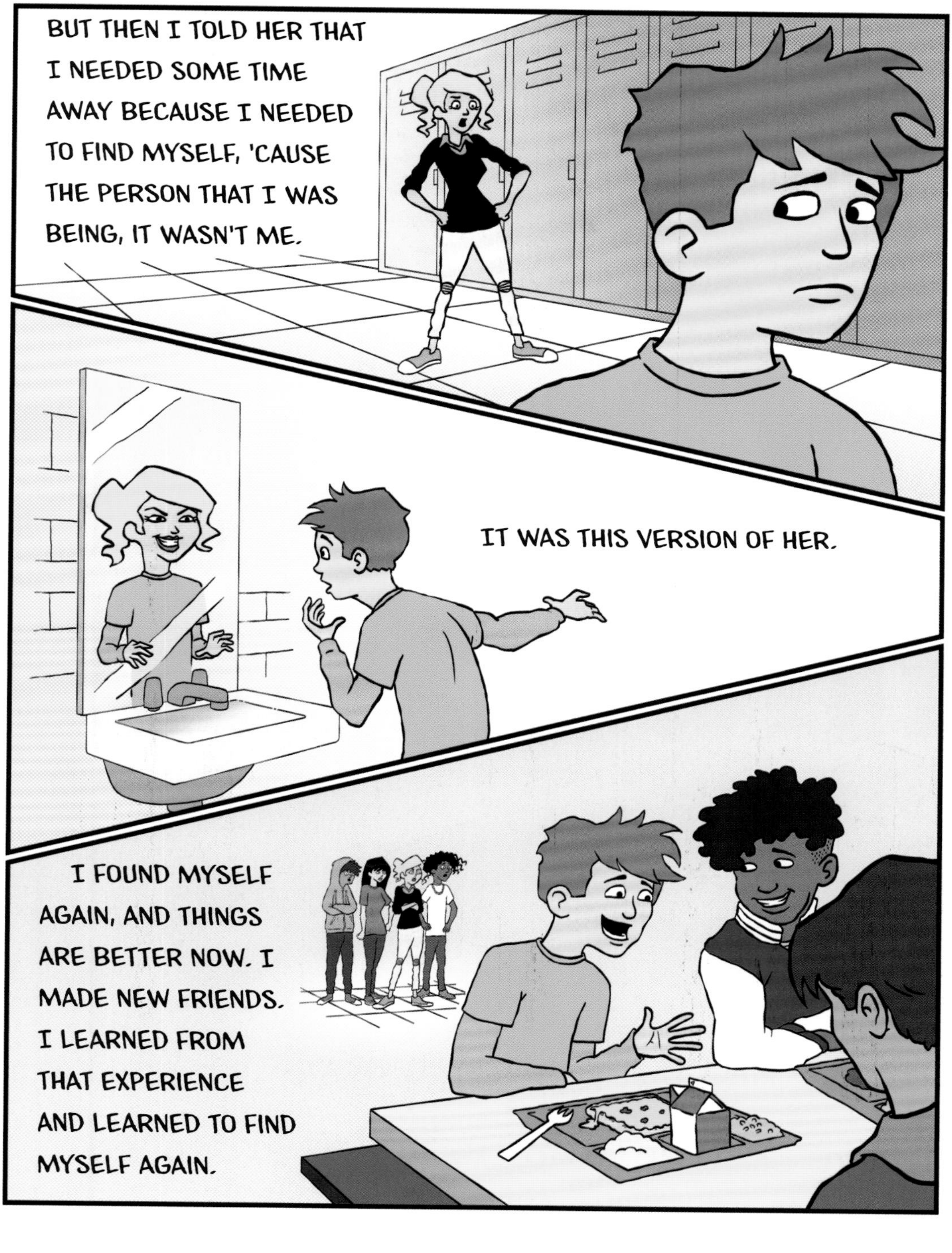
BUT THEN I TOLD HER THAT I NEEDED SOME TIME AWAY BECAUSE I NEEDED TO FIND MYSELF, 'CAUSE THE PERSON THAT I WAS BEING, IT WASN'T ME.
IT WAS THIS VERSION OF HER.
I FOUND MYSELF AGAIN, AND THINGS ARE BETTER NOW. I MADE NEW FRIENDS. I LEARNED FROM THAT EXPERIENCE AND LEARNED TO FIND MYSELF AGAIN.

I've been comparing myself to other girls since I was about eight and I don't know what to do. The girls in my class just seem so perfect.

Whenever

much mer

I let it out

I can barely keep my own head above water and yet I'm expected to help everyone else remain afloat.

It's been years since I've been bullied, but I still want an apology.

MY BEST FRIEND REPLACED ME.

I feel too tal pain, by crying.

On my first day of freshman year, I'm fresh out of middle school and I have no idea what I'm doing.

PEOPLE IN MY HOMETOWN DESPISED gay people. I tried to make myself look like the straightest person people ever knew because I was afraid to be judged.

MY FRIEND GAVE ME SOME pills. She said it would make us lose weight. It didn't really look legit to me, but at the time I was so desperate I'd do anything to shed the fat. So we both agreed to take the pills every morning. The first time I took the pill I started to experience heavy breathing and hot flashes. I felt extremely uncomfortable. I told my friend about it, and she was so excited. She told me it meant the pills were working, and I was very happy to hear that. Finally, I was going to lose weight! When I took it the second time, I felt so uncomfortable that I couldn't sleep and my body began shaking. I knew something was wrong, but I wasn't listening to my body. I—JUST—WANTED—TO—LOSE—WEIGHT. I kept taking them and taking them. Then one morning, I started feeling really dizzy and light and sleepy and weak all of a sudden. I don't know what happened, but when I woke up I was lying in a hospital bed with my mom by my side. In the days that followed, I was only fed with liquids because I couldn't eat anything. My mom burst into tears every time she came to visit me in the hospital. It broke my heart. I started to blame myself for everything. Everything became one big nightmare. It was really dark.

Now I'm better. I'm still healing, but I'm starting to feel more confident in myself.

WE WERE SO SCARED. OUR hearts were beating. Mind you, we're three black kids. We see what happens in the media every day when black people get pulled over.

I'm so worried because I want to go outside, **I WANT TO LIVE MY LIFE,** I want to be a teen, I want to spend time with my friends. But I can't do that when I'm worried that if I walk outside my house I'll get shot and killed just because of the color of my skin. **I'M SCARED. I'M SCARED OF SOCIETY. I'M SCARED OF HUMANITY. I'M SCARED OF PEOPLE. I'M SCARED OF THE COPS. I'M SCARED OF THE GOVERNMENT. I'M SCARED OF EVERYTHING.**

I can't help it that I was born a way that people hate.

THEN HE CONFESSED. HE WAS LIKE,

YOU KNOW, EVER SINCE THE FIRST DAY OF SCHOOL, I ACTUALLY HAD A THING FOR YOU.

AND I WAS LIKE,

OH MY GOD! I HAVE HAD A THING FOR YOU TOO.

AND THEN HE JUST PULLED ME IN AND KISSED ME. AND I STARTED KISSING BACK.

IN MY HEAD, I WAS LIKE, "OH MY GOD, MY CRUSH IS LITERALLY EXCHANGING SALIVA WITH ME."

ONE DAY I WAS HANGING OUT WITH FRIENDS AT A SLEEPOVER. WE WERE ALL GOING AROUND SAYING WHO WE HAD A CRUSH ON. IT TURNS OUT MY BEST FRIEND AND I HAD A CRUSH ON THE SAME GUY.

MY BEST FRIEND KNEW MY PHONE PASSWORD, AND I USED THE SAME PASSWORD FOR PRETTY MUCH EVERYTHING. SHE TOOK MY PHONE WITHOUT ME KNOWING AND TEXTED OUR CRUSH.

SHE TEXTED HIM MEAN THINGS TO TRY TO SABOTAGE MY CHANCES WITH HIM. WHEN I LOOKED AT MY PHONE, I SAW THESE TEXTS THAT I DIDN'T WRITE.

I TOLD MY BEST FRIEND, AND SHE PRETENDED LIKE SHE HAD NO CLUE WHO WOULD HAVE TAKEN MY PHONE AND DONE THIS. I TOLD ALL MY FRIENDS, AND NONE OF THEM KNEW WHO IT WAS EITHER.

I FOUND OUT LATER THAT SOMEONE HAD GONE INTO MY ACCOUNT AGAIN AND TEXTED A BOY WHO LIKED ME, SAYING THAT I HATED HIM AND THINGS LIKE, "YOU'LL NEVER BE GOOD ENOUGH" AND "NO ONE LIKES YOU."

I COULDN'T FIGURE OUT WHAT WAS HAPPENING, AND PEOPLE WERE STARTING TO GET MAD AT ME, THINKING IT WAS ME. PEOPLE STOPPED BEING MY FRIEND.

IT SEEMED LIKE MY BEST FRIEND WAS MY ONLY FRIEND AT THAT TIME, BUT I DIDN'T KNOW THAT SHE WAS THE ONE TAKING MY PHONE AND DOING THESE THINGS.

ONE DAY, I FOUND OUT IT WAS HER BECAUSE SHE HAD TAKEN PICTURES ON MY PHONE IN MY SNAPCHAT AND STARTED POSTING THEM, SAYING, "ADD ME," BUT SHE PUT IN HER USERNAME BY MISTAKE. I CONFRONTED HER AND ASKED HER WHY SHE DID THESE THINGS AND TOLD HER SHE NEEDED TO STOP. SHE JUST SAID NO. I WAS SHOCKED AND SO HURT. HOW COULD MY BEST FRIEND DO THIS TO ME?

I MADE A WHOLE NEW ACCOUNT AND BLOCKED HER ON EVERYTHING.

THAT SUMMER I MOVED, SO I DON'T HAVE TO SEE HER ANYMORE, BUT IT STILL REALLY HURTS.

JUST MAKE SURE THAT YOU DON'T EVER GIVE AWAY YOUR PASSWORD.

HE GRABBED MY ARM AND SAID,

WHERE ARE YOU GOING?

AND I SAID,

TO LOOK FOR MY PARENTS.

DON'T GO YET.

AND HE PULLED ME CLOSER, SAYING,

AND I DIDN'T REALLY KNOW WHAT WAS HAPPENING. I MEAN, I WAS TEN. I HADN'T EVEN KISSED A BOY YET.

AND THEN I JUST FELT SOMETHING COME UP BETWEEN MY LEGS, AND I HAD NO CLUE WHAT WAS HAPPENING BECAUSE I DIDN'T EVEN KNOW WHAT IT WAS. AND HE JUST PUSHED ME AGAINST THE WALL.

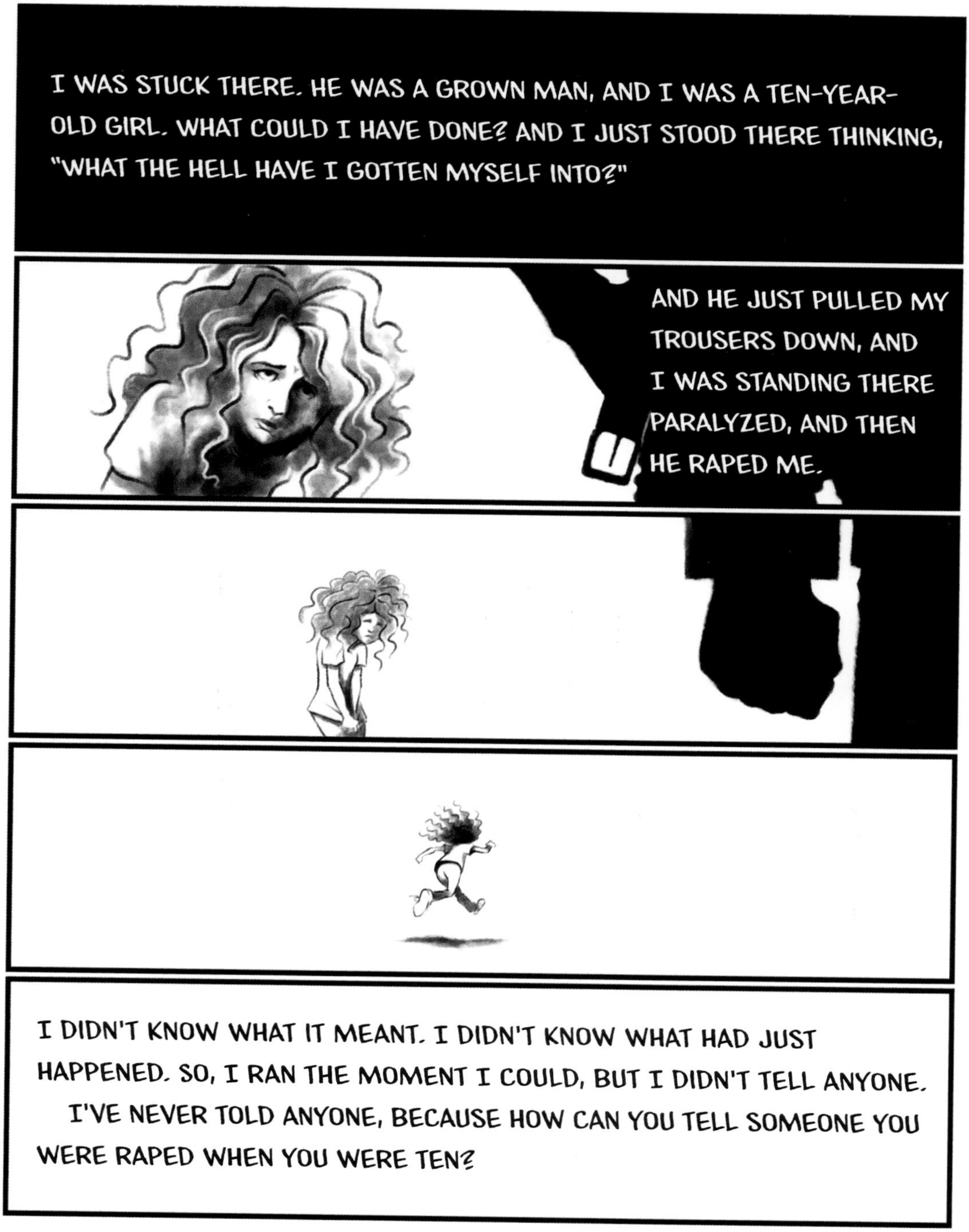
I WAS STUCK THERE. HE WAS A GROWN MAN, AND I WAS A TEN-YEAR-OLD GIRL. WHAT COULD I HAVE DONE? AND I JUST STOOD THERE THINKING, "WHAT THE HELL HAVE I GOTTEN MYSELF INTO?"
AND HE JUST PULLED MY TROUSERS DOWN, AND I WAS STANDING THERE PARALYZED, AND THEN HE RAPED ME.
I DIDN'T KNOW WHAT IT MEANT. I DIDN'T KNOW WHAT HAD JUST HAPPENED. SO, I RAN THE MOMENT I COULD, BUT I DIDN'T TELL ANYONE.
I'VE NEVER TOLD ANYONE, BECAUSE HOW CAN YOU TELL SOMEONE YOU WERE RAPED WHEN YOU WERE TEN?

I FINALL

COURAG

my SECRE

GLAD

got THE

TO TELL

AND
I'M really

I did.

IN EIGHTH GRADE, I HAD MY FIRST BOYFRIEND. SO I WAS ABOUT TO LEAVE FOR A SUMMER CAMP, AND WE SAID GOODBYE. IT WAS A LITTLE SAD BECAUSE I KNEW I WOULDN'T BE SEEING HIM FOR NINE WEEKS.

SO I WENT TO THIS CAMP. THERE WAS THIS BOY, AND HE SAID THAT HE REALLY LIKED ME. I DIDN'T KNOW WHAT TO DO BECAUSE HE WAS VERY ATTRACTIVE, AND HE WAS KIND OF A BAD BOY, LIKE, ONE OF THOSE COOL BAD BOYS. I WAS NOTICING MYSELF CATCHING FEELS FOR HIM, AND I WAS WORRIED. I DIDN'T WANT ANYTHING BAD TO HAPPEN BECAUSE OF MY BOYFRIEND.

I GOT PUT ON A FIVE-DAY OVERNIGHT TRIP WITH THE BOY. ON THE TRIP I WAS HANGING OUT WITH HIM FOR A BIT, AND I NOTICED MYSELF KIND OF CATCHING FEELINGS SOME MORE, AND I WAS LIKE,

NO, THIS CAN'T HAPPEN.

ONE NIGHT ON THE TRIP, WE HAD THE LONGEST CONVERSATION WHILE EVERYONE WAS SLEEPING, AND HE SAID,

I REALLY WANT TO KISS YOU.

AND ME, BEING REALLY NAIVE AND NOT KNOWING WHAT TO DO, AND ALSO KIND OF BEING LIKE "YES! HE WANTS TO KISS ME!" I JUST SAID, "OKAY." AND SO HE DID, AND THAT WAS THAT.

SO, THE NEXT COUPLE DAYS I FELT SO TERRIBLE ABOUT MYSELF. THIS TERRIBLE GUILT JUST CARRIED ON THROUGHOUT THE REST OF CAMP.

WHEN I GOT HOME, I DECIDED TO BE HONEST WITH MY BOYFRIEND, AND HE SEEMED TO BE PRETTY OKAY WITH IT. BUT I BROKE UP WITH HIM ANYWAY BECAUSE I FELT SO GUILTY.

EVERY TIME I SAW HIM, IT REMINDED ME OF WHAT A TERRIBLE PERSON I WAS.

LOOKING BACK ON IT, IT WAS A KISS, AND I COULD HAVE APPROACHED IT IN SO MANY OTHER WAYS INSTEAD OF BEATING MYSELF OVER THE HEAD FOR SOMETHING I WAS TOO IMMATURE TO DEAL WITH.

I get picked on

because I am

OVERWEIGHT.

I WAS IN THE NINTH grade, and because of the coronavirus I was in online school. One day in French class, my teacher decided to set us up in groups to work on a project together, so she put us in breakout rooms of five to six students.

Basically, I have a cat who doesn't really meow unless he's hungry or something. So sometimes I just randomly meow at him, even though I know he's not going to meow back. So, I'm in my Zoom class and my mic is on and I didn't know it. I wasn't paying attention. So, I was very stupid and decided to make the weirdest sounds ever. I was roaring, I was meowing, I was stretching at the same time, and I sounded extremely stupid and cringey. And I looked at my screen and saw that my mic was on, so everybody in the breakout room heard me, including my teacher, who was peeping over the Zoom.

I was so embarrassed. Everybody heard, and everybody was extremely weirded out. Moral of the story? Do not meow at your cats, and always look at your screen to see if your mic is on or off in a Zoom class.

Bad things felt never-ending. I kept to myself until I opened up to my Mom and got help.

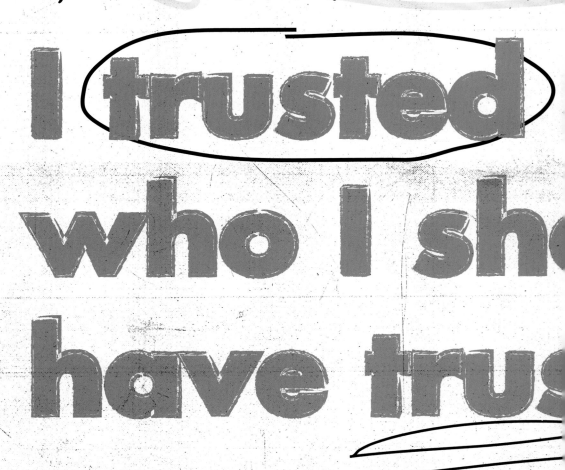

I trusted who I should have trusted

omeone
ouldn't
ted.

MY GIRLFRIEND BROKE UP WITH ME AND I CAN'T EVEN CRY. I TRY TO SHOW EMOTION BUT I CAN'T, WHICH MAKES ME NOT LIKE MYSELF.

I DRANK FOR THE FIRST time when I was fourteen. I stole some alcohol from a bottle of wine my parents had in the fridge. It was just one glass. I didn't even get drunk, but I woke up the next morning craving it again and obsessing over it. I didn't drink again for a while, but then when I was sixteen, I started drinking regularly. I stole all the wine my parents had in the cabinets. They rarely drank, so they had no idea. And I was good at acting sober around them.

My grades started plummeting, and I wasn't taking school seriously. I wasn't taking anything in my life seriously. I was just being self-destructive. Then on Valentine's Day my parents left me alone for the weekend. I ordered a pizza, got a bottle of wine, and ended up much too drunk and in the hospital. My parents were called and had to come back from their trip early. Even though I quit drinking after that, I spent eighteen months being what most people call a dry drunk. I wasn't drinking but I also wasn't doing anything to recover, deal with my problems, or find out why I wanted alcohol so badly.

I guess I felt like my situation or how much I drank wasn't bad enough to reach out for help, which wasn't true.

I also believed that I was too young to be an actual alcoholic, which again wasn't true. Finally, one night, eighteen months after I quit drinking, I was talking to a friend about how I was considering relapsing. She told me, "You need to get help now." For some reason, that was when it clicked for me that I couldn't do it alone anymore. So, I looked up Alcoholics Anonymous meetings happening around me. I went to my first Alcoholics Anonymous meeting, and I was terrified. I was the youngest person there by far, but everybody just surrounded me with love. They cared about me, and I was welcomed with open arms. That was the day I got my sponsor and started working on my recovery.

I've since done the 12 Steps and experienced amazing changes in my life. I want my story to inspire other young alcoholics or addicts to reach out and get help, because you cannot do it alone. You cannot be sober by yourself. You need to get help, and there is no shame in getting help.

With abuse you think of hitting with blunt-force objects, either fists or pipes. You think of throwing and grabbing and screaming, but in reality, it's **SOMETHING MUCH, MUCH DARKER** and more sinister. You are born and raised in an environment, and you think it is normal your entire life. You've known nothing else. So when things happen you don't think much of it—your dad calling you a bitch, a slut—you don't think much of it. **IT HURTS**, but you think everybody goes through it, so **YOU JUST KEEP ON GOING.**

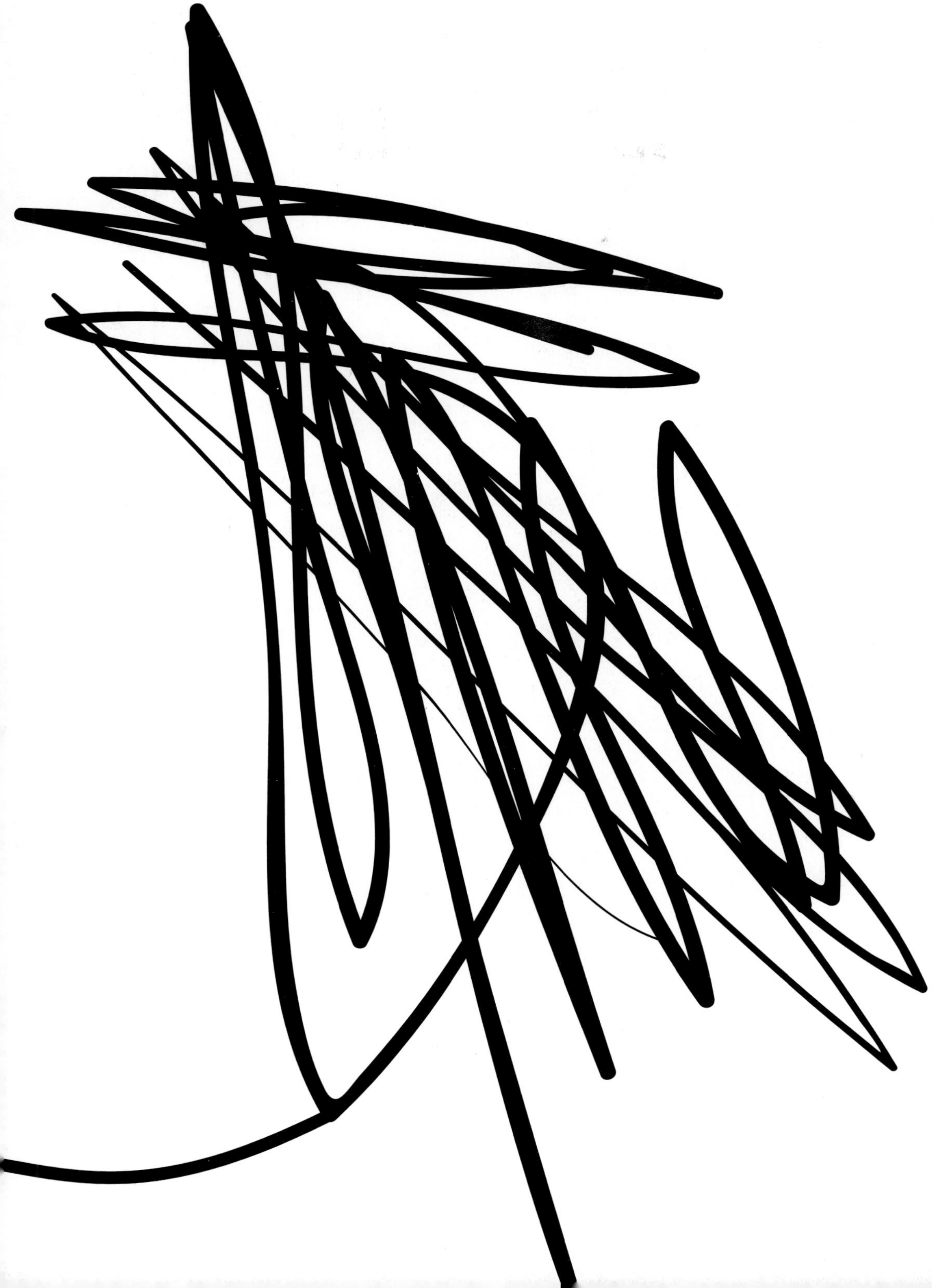

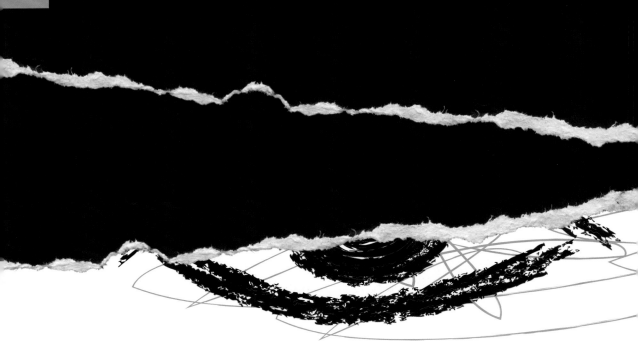

My stepfather made me watch things that I wasn't supposed to watch and it made me stressed. It made me sad. **IT MADE ME SHAKY INSIDE AND SCARED.** He tried to hurt me when my mom was away. He'd do things he wasn't supposed to. Things

that could get you a lifetime in jail. But I couldn't say anything. **I DIDN'T WANNA GET IN TROUBLE. SO I KEPT MY MOUTH SHUT.** But finally, finally, finally, I knew I had to tell my mom. So I went to her and told her what happened.

BECAUSE
I'M YO
DOE
I'M
STR

OUNG

N'T MEAN

NOT

ONG.

FRESHMAN YEAR I HAD MY FIRST BOYFRIEND, AND IT WAS PRETTY AMAZING. WE DATED FOR FOUR MONTHS, AND THEN, OUT OF NOWHERE, HE ASKS, "UM, DO YOU WANT TO HAVE SEX?"

YES, SEX. I DIDN'T REALLY KNOW WHAT TO DO WITH THAT. I MEAN, I WAS THINKING, DO NORMAL TEENAGE RELATIONSHIPS START LIKE THIS? BUT I WAS LIKE, "OKAY, LET'S DO IT."

IT WAS THE WEEKEND, AND HE WAS READY TO DO IT, SO WE WENT TO THE PARK. I WAS HAVING LOTS OF THOUGHTS ON EVERYTHING.

I HONESTLY WAS THINKING, "WHAT DO I TELL MY MOM, LIKE HOW I LOST MY VIRGINITY? DO I TELL HER THAT I LOST IT AT THE PARK FRESHMAN YEAR? YEAH--I DON'T THINK SO."

SO I CHANGED MY MIND. I SAID, "I DO NOT WANT TO DO THIS."

AND THIS DUDE TRIES TO PRESSURE ME. HE ASKS AND PLEADS, SAYING,

PLEASE, I REALLY WANT TO DO THIS WITH YOU,

AND I WAS JUST LIKE,

LET'S JUST WAIT UNTIL WE'RE OLDER, BECAUSE I'M NOT READY.

THEN, NOT MUCH LATER ON, HE BROKE UP WITH ME. I WAS SO UPSET. I WAS CRYING FOREVER BECAUSE IT WAS MY FIRST LOVE AND, WELL, I DON'T EVEN KNOW WHAT LOVE IS, SO I DON'T KNOW.

I HAD A BEST FRIEND, AND WE DID EVERYTHING TOGETHER. SHE JUST MADE ME A BETTER PERSON, AND I LOVED HER SO MUCH. ONE DAY I WAS HANGING WITH HER WHEN MY OTHER TWO FRIENDS CAME UP TO ME

AND SAID, "COME HERE." THEN THEY TOLD ME,

UNLESS YOU WANT TO NOT BE FRIENDS WITH US ANYMORE, YOU HAVE TO GO TELL YOUR FRIEND THAT SHE CANNOT BE FRIENDS WITH YOU ANYMORE. SHE DOESN'T BELONG HERE BECAUSE SHE IS MUSLIM.

SO ME, THINKING THAT I NEED TO BE POPULAR AND I NEED TO BE LIKED BY MORE PEOPLE, WENT UP TO MY FRIEND AND, FEELING SO GUILTY,

I TOLD HER THAT I COULDN'T BE FRIENDS WITH HER ANYMORE AND THAT SHE DIDN'T BELONG HERE, AND THAT HER CULTURE WASN'T GOOD.

I TOLD HER SHE SHOULD JUST GO HOME BECAUSE NOBODY LIKED HER.
AND I FELT SO BAD, AND I WAS MAD AT MYSELF FOR DOING THAT TO HER, BECAUSE IT WAS SO AWFUL WHAT I DID.

AND AS I WAS HANGING OUT WITH MY TWO FRIENDS, I JUST DIDN'T BELONG WITH THEM BECAUSE THEY JUST WEREN'T GOOD PEOPLE. THEY JUST DIDN'T FIT WITH ME LIKE MY BEST FRIEND DID. I MISSED MY BEST FRIEND SO MUCH.

I WAS JUST SO SCARED TO GO UP TO HER AND TELL HER THAT I MISSED HER, AND THAT I WAS SO SORRY FOR WHAT I HAD DONE. SHE MADE NEW FRIENDS, AND I DIDN'T FEEL LIKE SHE WANTED TO BE MY FRIEND ANYMORE.

BUT I WENT UP TO HER AND TOLD HER HOW SORRY I WAS, BUT SHE DIDN'T BELIEVE ME.

AND FOR WEEKS I KEPT TELLING HER I WAS SORRY UNTIL FINALLY SHE FORGAVE ME.

WE HAVE BEEN BEST FRIENDS EVER SINCE. AND WE'RE EVEN BETTER NOW THAN EVER BEFORE. I STILL CAN'T BELIEVE THAT I DID THAT TO HER AND STILL FEEL GUILTY.

BEING LIKE ME ISN'T EASY. IT'S LIKE I'VE BEEN THROWN IN THE OCEAN.

IT'S COLD AND I'M ALONE, AND I DON'T THINK I CAN SWIM MUCH LONGER.

THERE'S BEEN PLENTY OF TIMES WHERE I'VE CUT MYSELF AND I'VE THOUGHT ABOUT KILLING MYSELF.

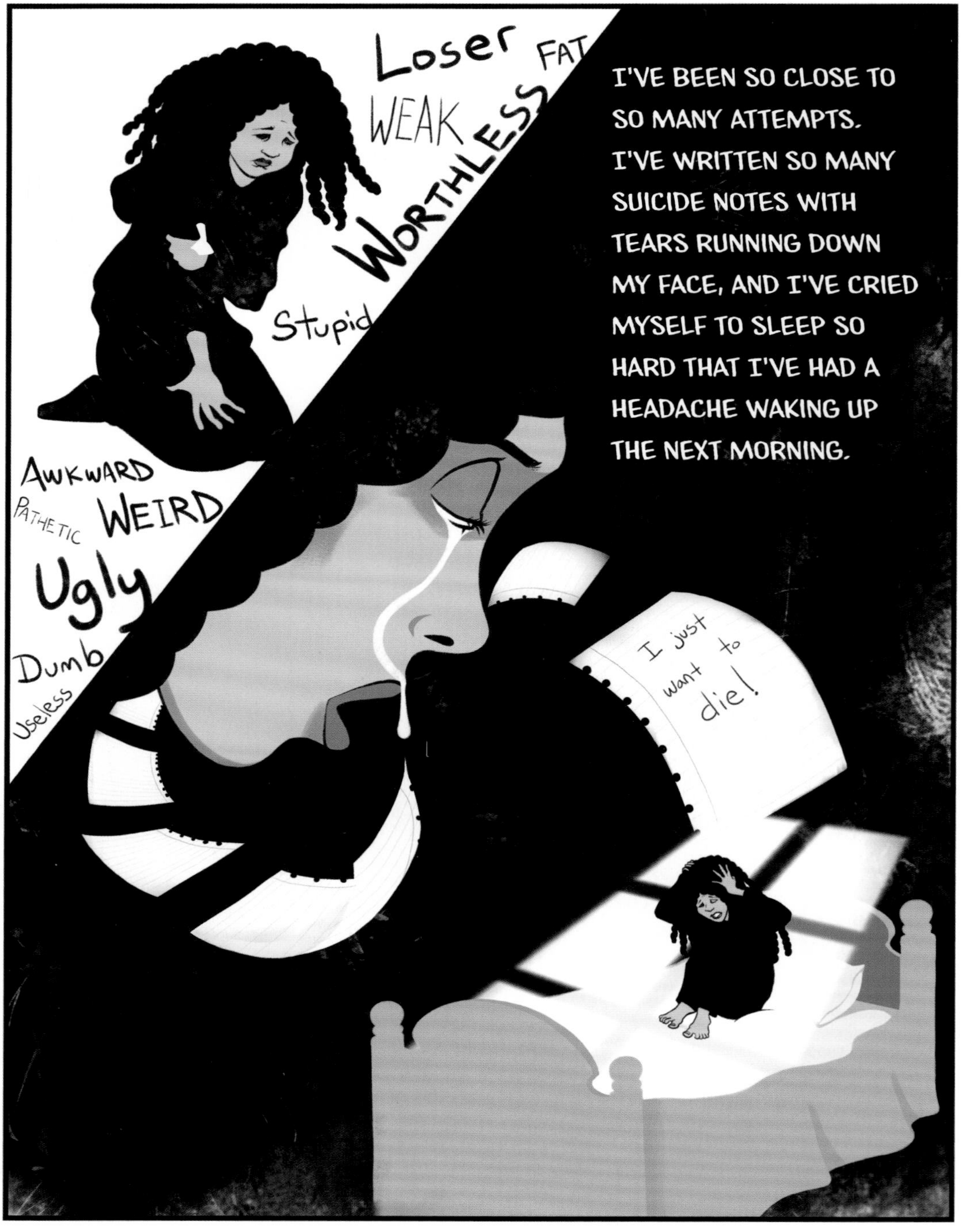
Loser
FAT
WEAK
WORTHLESS
Stupid
AWKWARD
PATHETIC
WEIRD
Ugly
Dumb
Useless
I'VE BEEN SO CLOSE TO SO MANY ATTEMPTS. I'VE WRITTEN SO MANY SUICIDE NOTES WITH TEARS RUNNING DOWN MY FACE, AND I'VE CRIED MYSELF TO SLEEP SO HARD THAT I'VE HAD A HEADACHE WAKING UP THE NEXT MORNING.
I just want to die!

BUT I'VE JUST GOT TO KEEP ON TRUCKING TILL I SEE THE LIGHT AT THE END OF THE TUNNEL, AND I'VE GOT TO KEEP REMINDING MYSELF OF THAT, AND I WANT TO REMIND EVERYBODY ELSE OF THAT TOO. YOU CAN'T JUST STOP. YOU CAN'T LIE DOWN AT THE END OF THE ROAD, AND YOU CAN'T JUST GIVE UP.

THERE'S MORE, AND THERE'S GOING TO BE SO MUCH MORE. THERE ARE THINGS THAT YOU HAVEN'T EXPERIENCED. THERE ARE THINGS THAT PEOPLE STILL HAVEN'T FOUND OR THINGS THAT YOU HAVEN'T SEEN, AND YET YOU'RE STARTING TO GIVE UP ON SOMETHING THAT HASN'T EVEN REALLY BEGUN YET.

I have dys
and it can
hard. I ge
at by ever

My real dad saw me in public by
accident for the first time. He
looked at me like I didn't exist. :/

My mom always tries to plan my life the way she wants my life to go. She doesn't understand that she had her time to do what she wants and now it's my turn to do my life.

exia

get pretty

laughed

one.

THERE ARE PEOPLE IN OUR LIVES THAT MAKE US FEEL SAFE AND LOVED AND RESPECTED, AND THEN, FOR SOME OF US OUT THERE, THERE ARE PEOPLE IN OUR LIVES THAT ARE SUPPOSED TO MAKE US FEEL SAFE AND LOVED AND RESPECTED, BUT THEY DON'T DO THEIR JOB.

FROM A YOUNG AGE, I WAS ALWAYS RIDICULED, TEASED, AND TAUNTED BY MY MOM. I GREW UP WITH A VERY LOW SELF-ESTEEM BECAUSE MY MOM WOULD SAY THINGS LIKE,

YOU'RE TERRIBLE.

I DON'T LIKE YOU.
I DON'T LOVE YOU AT ALL.

I THINK THAT YOU'RE A BIG BURDEN TO THIS FAMILY. WHAT SIN COULD I HAVE POSSIBLY COMMITTED TO HAVE HAD YOU AS A KID?

AND SHE THOUGHT THAT ALL OF THESE WORDS WOULD JUST BRUSH OVER ME, AND THAT I WOULD SOMEHOW REALIZE THAT SHE DIDN'T MEAN THEM.

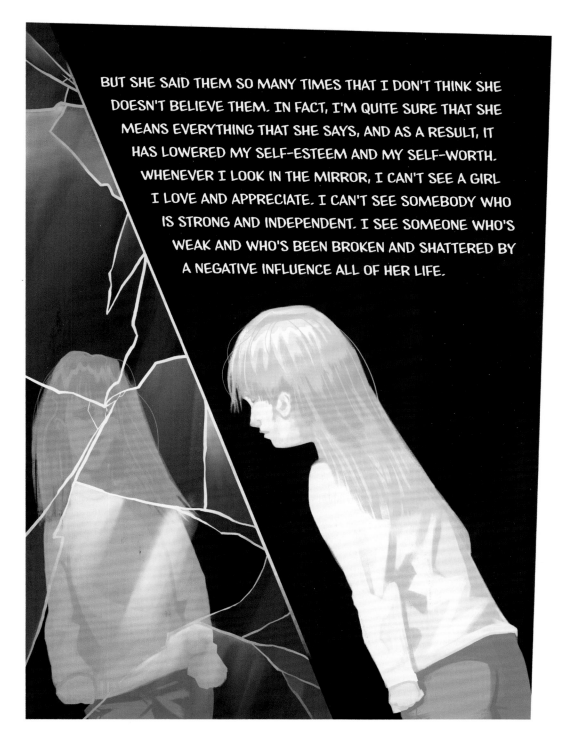

BUT SHE SAID THEM SO MANY TIMES THAT I DON'T THINK SHE DOESN'T BELIEVE THEM. IN FACT, I'M QUITE SURE THAT SHE MEANS EVERYTHING THAT SHE SAYS, AND AS A RESULT, IT HAS LOWERED MY SELF-ESTEEM AND MY SELF-WORTH. WHENEVER I LOOK IN THE MIRROR, I CAN'T SEE A GIRL I LOVE AND APPRECIATE. I CAN'T SEE SOMEBODY WHO IS STRONG AND INDEPENDENT. I SEE SOMEONE WHO'S WEAK AND WHO'S BEEN BROKEN AND SHATTERED BY A NEGATIVE INFLUENCE ALL OF HER LIFE.

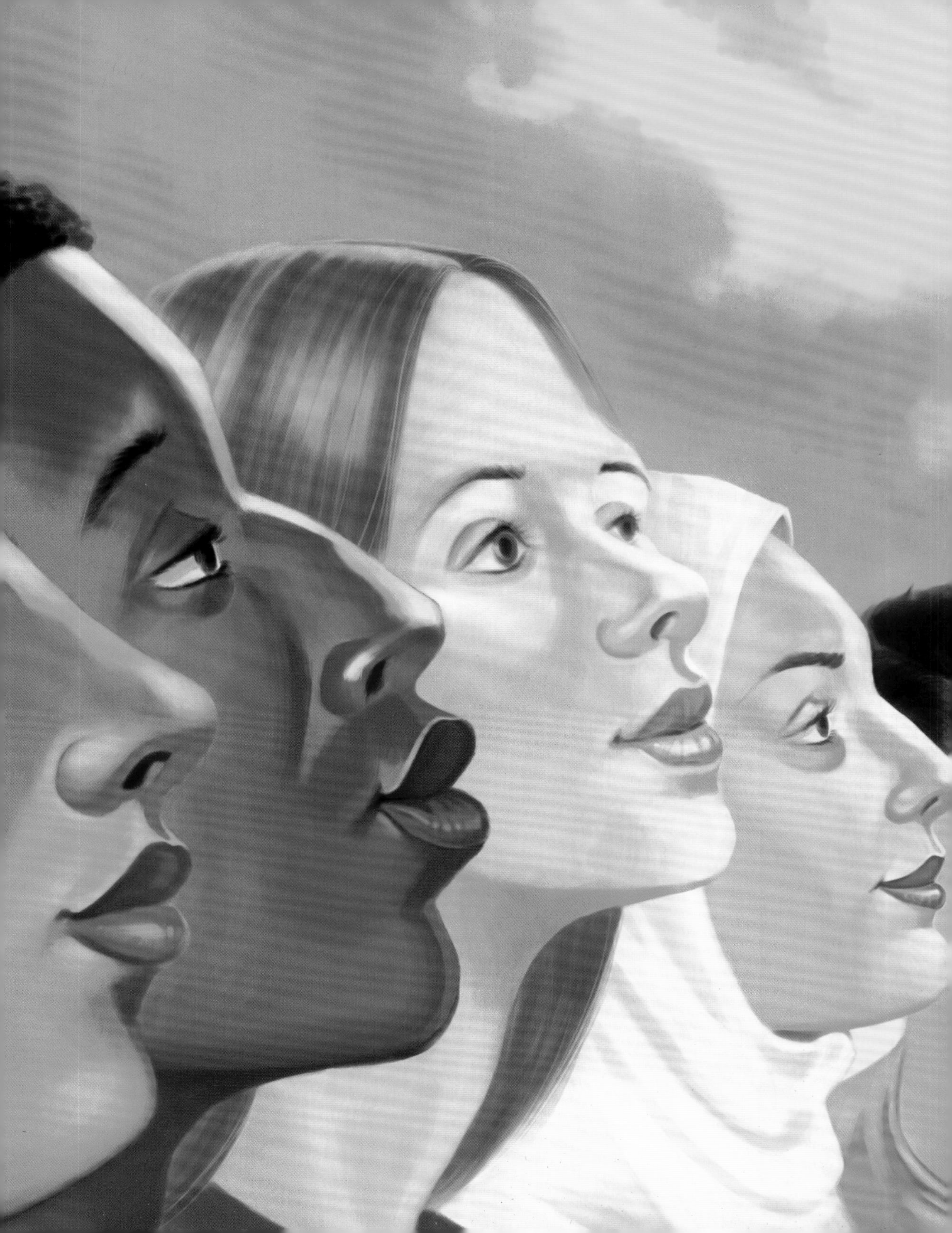

To those of you out there who are struggling because of some negative influence in your life, whether it be your parents or an ex-best friend or an ex-boyfriend or a bully or anything, please remember that you're not alone, you don't deserve to suffer this way.

YOU ARE WONDERFUL, PASSIONATE HUMAN BEINGS, AND YOU HAVE SO MUCH TO OFFER THIS WORLD.

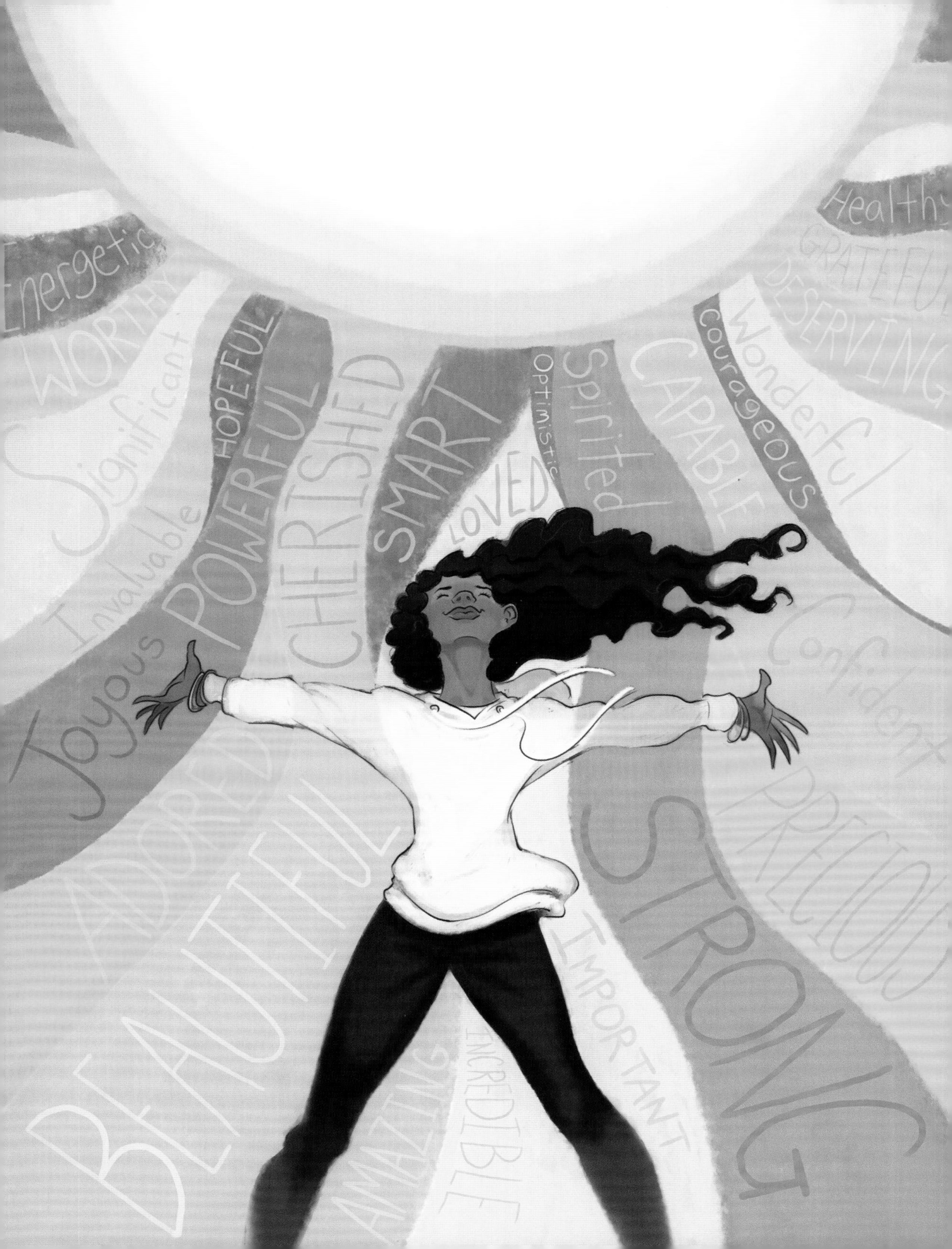
WORTHY
Significant
Invaluable
Joyous
HOPEFUL
POWERFUL
CHERISHED
SMART
LOVED
Optimistic
Spirited
CAPABLE
courageous
Wonderful
DESERVING
Confident
STRONG
IMPORTANT
INCREDIBLE
AMAZING
BEAUTIFUL

You are
WORTH
EVERY-
THING.

We know it can be scary and uncomfortable to ask for help if you are struggling, but you don't need to be alone in what you are going through.

Don't be afraid to ask for help from a trusted person in your life (like a parent, teacher, or guidance counselor). If there is no one you know who you feel comfortable sharing with, we put together a list of places that you can feel safe reaching out to for support.

It's courageous to ask for help, and it's the first step to feeling better. We know you can do it. ☺

RESOURCES

National Alliance on Mental Illness (NAMI)
www.nami.org
1-800-950-NAMI
The NAMI HelpLine is a free service that provides information, referrals, and support to people living with a mental health condition, family members and caregivers, mental health providers and the public.

National Domestic Violence Hotline
www.thehotline.org
1-800-799-7233
The Hotline is the only 24/7 center in the nation that has access to service providers and shelters across the U.S.

National Sexual Violence Resource Center
www.nsvrc.org
1-717-909-0710
The National Sexual Violence Resource Center (NSVRC) is the leading nonprofit in providing information and tools to prevent and respond to sexual violence.

Planned Parenthood
www.plannedparenthood.org
1-800-230-PLAN
Planned Parenthood is a trusted health care provider, educator, and passionate advocate. Each year, Planned Parenthood delivers vital sexual and reproductive health care, sex education, and information to millions of people.

RAINN

www.rainn.org

RAINN (Rape, Abuse & Incest National Network) is the nation's largest anti-sexual violence organization. RAINN created and operates the National Sexual Assault Hotline (800.656.HOPE, www.online.rainn.org and www.rainn.org/es) in partnership with more than 1,000 local sexual assault service providers across the country and operates the DoD Safe Helpline for the Department of Defense. RAINN also carries out programs to prevent sexual violence, help survivors, and ensure that perpetrators are brought to justice.

SAMHSA National Helpline

www.samhsa.gov

1-800-662-HELP

SAMHSA's National Helpline is a confidential, free, 24-hour-a-day, 365-day-a-year, information service, in English and Spanish, for individuals and family members facing mental and/or substance use disorders.

Suicide Prevention Lifeline

www.suicidepreventionlifeline.org

1-800-273-8255

The National Suicide Prevention Lifeline provides free and confidential emotional support to people in suicidal crisis or emotional distress 24 hours a day, 7 days a week, across the United States.

The Trevor Project

www.thetrevorproject.org

1-866-488-7386

The Trevor Project is the leading national organization providing crisis intervention and suicide prevention services to lesbian, gay, bisexual, transgender, queer, & questioning (LGBTQ) young people under 25.